URP GCOE DOCUMENT 11

Creating Cities;
Culture, Space and Sustainability:
The 1st City, Culture and Society (CCS) Conference

大阪市立大学 都市研究プラザ
Urban Research Plaza, Osaka City University

© 2012 Urban Research Plaza, Osaka City University

All rights reserved. No part of this publication may be reproduced, stored in a retrieval system, or transmitted, in any form or by any means, electronic, mechanical, photocopying, recording, or otherwise, without the prior written permission of the publisher.

URP GCOE DOCUMENT 11
Creating Cities;
Culture, Space and Sustainability:
The 1st City, Culture and Society (CCS) Conference
Editors: Evelyn Schulz and Hiroshi Okano

Published by Urban Research Plaza, Osaka City University
3-3-138, Sugimoto, Sumiyoshi-ku, Osaka, 558-8585 JAPAN
Tel:+81-6-6605-2071
Fax:+81-6-6605-2069
www.ur-plaza.osaka-cu.ac.jp

ISBN 978-4-904010-12-9
Printed in Japan

Contents

Introduction ... 4
Evelyn Schulz and Hiroshi Okano

Contributors ... 8

I. *Creative Diversity, Socioscapes, and Cultural Politics*

1. Spaces of Poverty, Spaces of Prosperity: Incomplete Tourist Encounters in Mexico ... 12
Eveline Dürr

2. Creating Creative Cities?: Cultural Administration and Local Authorities in Japan since the 1970s ... 20
Mari Kobayashi

3. Projects of Creativity and Inclusion: The Challenges of Cultural Development in Mexico City ... 28
Ana Rosas Mantecón

4. Revitalizing Tokyo's Back Alleys as Areas of Cultural Sustainability and a Decelerated Lifestyle ... 34
Evelyn Schulz

5. Creativity Starts Here: Rotterdam (NL): Creative Citizens Meet Creative City Policies ... 46
Lidewij Tummers

II. *Networks, Mobility and Built Environment*

6. From Growth to Quality: Less is Future ... 56
Sonja Beeck

7. Mobility in the In-between City: Getting Stuck between the Local and the Global ... 62
Roger Keil

8. Neoliberal Hypermobility and the Tricycle ... 70
Glen Norcliffe

9. Finding a Place for Japanese and Chinese Cities within an East Asian Regional Urbanism ... 78
Paul Waley

10. Mediating a Global Network in Crisis: *The New York Times* Maps the Moral Geography of Global Finance ... 92
Gordon M. Winder

Introduction

Evelyn Schulz and Hiroshi Okano

For the first time in history more than half of all humans live in towns and cities. Urban growth is substantially transforming the face of the planet. On the one hand, there is clear evidence that in certain areas urban growth is coming to a close and cities have actually entered a process of shrinkage. Prominent examples are to be found in Japan and in Germany. On the other hand, there are many regions in the world that are still witnessing rampant urban growth. In the last decades, many buzzwords have emerged as part of the debate on the successful road to a well-balanced urban growth model. Many of these buzzwords such as sustainability, liveability, and last but not least, creativity run the latent risk of becoming devoid of all meaning due to overuse.

The term *creative city* is commonly associated with Charles Landry (*The Creative City: A Toolkit for Urban Innovators*, 2000 and *The Art of City Making*, 2006) and Richard Florida (*The Rise of the Creative Class*, 2002; *Cities and the Creative Class*, 2005; and *The Flight of the Creative Class*, 2005). According to their theories, those branches of economy that rely on artistic-cultural ideas and the resulting products will play an increasingly important role for the economic and social revitalization of transformed, post-industrial urban regions. The deeper the structural changes and accompanying problems are that a city faces, the more important its so-called *creative industries* become, according to Landry and Florida. They see the recent international financial meltdown as an important contributor to the acceleration of exactly those changes for the worse that *creative industries* may help to fight.

As diverse as the international debate on the concept or, rather, the concepts, of a *creative city* is, there is one common element. *Creativity*, broadly defined, is seen as a key element for urban development. Since a pluralistic society is a prerequisite of creativity, the hopes are high that creative industries can facilitate social integration, as can be seen by the Urban Research Plaza of Osaka City University's focus on 'Reinventing the City for Cultural Creativity and Social Inclusion'.

The papers gathered here are the outcome of *Creating Cities; Culture, Space and Sustainability: The 1st City, Culture and Society (CCS) Conference* which took place in Munich, Germany, February 25-27, 2010, and was organized by Evelyn Schulz (Japan Center, LMU Munich) in cooperation with Eveline Dürr (Institute for Cultural and Social Anthropology, LMU Munich), Irene Goetz (Institute for European Ethnology, LMU Munich), Franz Waldenberger (Japan Center, LMU Munich), Gordon Winder (Seminar of Economic History, LMU Munich), and the Urban Research Plaza of Osaka City University.

The term *creativity* seems to bridge a conceptual gap that is the result of challenges posed by today's demand for sustainable urban development strategies. Accordingly, the point of the conference was not so much to examine individual urban creative industries projects. Considering the many different urban development issues, such as shrinking resources, (in)stability, and rampant urban growth, the conference, rather, attempted to shed light on the heterogeneous forces at work and tried to forecast possible future developments.

The conference approached the multifaceted and rather controversial *creative city* debate from various points of view. The conference's goal was to analyze the economic, social, political, and cultural requirements for urban development as well as the global dimension of such processes. The conference focused on the following questions: As far as urban development is concerned, how do growth, on one hand, and the necessity for social and ecological Sustainability, on the other hand, interact? How does a created environment affect social space? How should a city be in order to promote creativity? When it comes right down to it, what actually is *creativity*? Which impact does cultural diversity have on the creative output? How do cities approach social and cultural diversity? How do their strategies influence creative activity? Do these kinds of strategies mean a risk too or are they rather the engine behind an economically and socially sustainable urban development? How far can political forces really create a *creative city*, an urban environment that encourages innovation and economic growth? These and similar questions were discussed by means of a wide range of case studies from all over the world and pertaining to a diverse range of fields of study.

Originally, the conference was divided into five sessions:

1) *Creative Cities & Creating Cities*

As global market forces penetrate hitherto closed rural areas wherever market liberalization occurs, urbanization, too, is progressing rapidly. Even though regional differences obviously do exist the global ratio of urban population has now crossed the 50-percent line. While mega cities may be one of the most conspicuous phenomena of the present urbanization the term urban must be understood in a much broader sense. The fact that the majority of urban dwellers still lives in smaller and medium-sized settlements is frequently overlooked. Only through a combined effort of local supplier development, national institutional support, and foreign investment can there be any real benefits from for example creative cluster development and economies of scale and scope. Two prominent regions of Southeast Asia, namely the Greater Mekong Region and Singapore, served as examples to investigate the relationship between the process of creating cities and the making of creative cities.

2) *Creative Diversity, Socioscapes, and Cultural Politics*

This session critically reviewed current notions and implications of cultural diversity in cities by bringing together broadly three strands: representation, socioscapes, and cultural politics. The interplay between creating particular urban images and the urban condition of particular socioscapes, ranging from less empowered groups such as those that are affected by transnational precarization to elite diasporas, was examined.

3) *Networks*

Global cities rely upon networks with other cities, and the institutions, infrastructure, character, extent and effects of such inter-city networking were the subject for this session. It identified the possibilities and constraints on such network development.

4) *Mobility and Built Environment*

Mobility is a crucial aspect of globalization and the development of more efficient mobility systems on a grand scale is a significant locus for planning activity in global cities. This session compared and contrasted corporate and planning approaches to mobility issues in several global cities.

5) *City Marketing*

Cities are increasingly undertaking marketing activities to support their local economy. By way of example, this section looked at how city marketing may cope with challenges in terms of communication content, tools or media, and with regard to underlying organizational structures and processes.

The working papers collected in this volume represent the thematic diversity of the conference and demonstrate the intense discussions. In particular the lively closing debate in which strengths and weaknesses of the concept of the *creative city* were discussed has led to many new insights and conclusions. In general, metropolitan cities with a rich cultural heritage seem to be the winners in the *creative city* paradigm. While it can hardly be denied that, even there, much of the allocated money is spent in order to create the illusion of innovation (for example, by means of flagship projects and events on a grand scale) it can nonetheless be observed that the local creative and cultural industries and their related institutions profit as well. New approaches to urban development have been advanced in order to increase the quality of life in targeted areas and to conserve local cultural traditions while strengthening cultural education. On the other hand, gentrification and social polarization can also be linked to the very same creative policies, which usually refuse to include the working class and immigrants altogether. It is the small- and medium-sized cities that were seen as the real losers of the *creative city* paradigm. More often than not, their only hope, it seems, is to tap into the economic and social benefits of an adjacent *creative capital*.

Contributors

Sonja BEECK is project manager at the Bauhaus Dessau Foundation, studied architecture, obtained her Ph.D. at the University of Karlsruhe (Theming: method of visual communication for semantic programming in the context of architecture and urban space). She was project manager for the International Building Exhibition "IBA Urban Redevelopment Saxony-Anhalt 2010". The project was set as a laboratory from 2002 until 2010. The focus of research and design was the question, how to develop new programs for shrinking cities and observe their spatial, social, cultural and economical consequences.

Eveline DÜRR is a Professor at the Institute of Social and Cultural Anthropology at the Ludwig-Maximilians-University in Munich, and previously held a position as Associate Professor in the School of Social Sciences, Auckland University of Technology, New Zealand. She received her PhD and *venia legendi* (Habilitation) from the University of Freiburg, Germany. She has conducted fieldwork in Mexico, the USA, Germany and New Zealand, and publishes on the urban environment, cultural identity formation and transnational linkages, especially between Latin America and the Pacific. Recently, she edited a volume with Rivke Jaffe, Leiden University, on *Urban Pollution: Cultural Meanings, Social Practices* (Berghahn Books, Oxford, 2010). In 2005, she published a book on urban Hispanic identities entitled *Identitaeten und Sinnbezuege in der Stadt. Hispanics im Suedwesten der USA*. Muenster: Lit.

Roger KEIL is the Director of the City Institute at York University, the Director of the Canadian Centre for German and European Studies, and Professor at the Faculty of Environmental Studies at York University, Toronto. Among his recent publications are *The Global Cities Reader* (London und New York: Routledge, 2006); ed. with S. Harris Ali, *Networked Disease: Emerging Infections and the Global City* (Oxford: Wiley-Blackwell, 2008); with Julie-Anne Boudreau and Douglas Young, *Changing Toronto: Governing the Neoliberal City* (Toronto: UTP, 2009); ed. with Rianne Mahon, *Leviathan Undone? The Political Economy of Scale* (Vancouver: UBC Press, 2009). His current research is on global suburbanism, infrastructure in the Zwischenstadt, on cities and infectious disease, and regional governance. Keil was the co-editor of the *International Journal of Urban and Regional Research* (*IJURR*) and a co-founder of the *International Network for Urban Research and Action* (*INURA*).

Mari KOBAYASHI is Associate Professor of Cultural Resources Studies (Graduate School of Humanities and Sociology) at the University of Tokyo. She is the author of *Toward Establishing the Cultural Rights: Comparative Studies about Cultural Promotion Law and Japanese Reality* (Japanese), Tokyo: Keiso Shobo, 2004. and "The Problem of Cultural Policy in the Globalization: The New Public Space in Germany (Japanese)" in *Globalization of Cultural*

Policy, Tokyo: Keiso Shobo 2009. She is also working with various local governments to implement cultural policies.

Glen NORCLIFFE is Professor Emeritus and Senior Scholar at York University in Toronto. For the past 40 years his research has focused on geographies of industry. Recent books include *The Ride to Modernity* (University of Toronto Press, 2001) and *Global Game, Local Arena* (ISER Books, 2005). His current work examines hypermobility in the global supply chains of the Canadian bicycle trade, the performance of trade shows, the impacts of neoliberalism on geographies of industry in general, and specifically on Canada's Green North during the phase of aggressive neoliberalism espoused by the "Common Sense Revolution". He is working on two books, one on geographies of industry and the other on the geographical construction of technology.

Hiroshi OKANO is a professor and vice-director of Urban Research Plaza, as well as a professor of Graduate School of Business, Osaka City University. He is the founding and managing editor of City, Culture and Society, Elsevier, and has served as an associate editor of Accounting, Auditing, Accountability Journal. He got his PhD from Osaka City University and visiting professor and scholar at LSE, Oxford, Stanford, ESSEC, etc. His research themes are strategic, historical, social and cultural aspects of strategic management accounting, financial management for private sectors, public sectors, music and art organizations, and recently, he is focusing at strategic and brand management for cities, urban development, poverty management, etc. He published papers in the international journals like Cities, Management Accounting Research, Accounting, Auditing, Accountability Journal, and books including Global Strategy & Accounting: International Comparison of R&D Management, Tokyo: Yuhikaku, 2003, Japanese management Accounting: A Historical & Institutional Perspectives, Tokyo Chuokeizaisha, 1995, 2nd edition, 2002, and "A History of Japanese Management Accounting," in Chapman, C. A.Hopwood & M.Shields (ed) Handbook of Management Accounting Research, Elsevier, so on. He was selected as a president of Academy of Accounting Historians in US (2007-2008).

Ana ROSAS MANTECON is anthropologist, full time teacher and researcher at Universidad Autónoma Metropolitana's Anthropology Department, Mexico, since 1992. Her research has specialized on cultural consumption and artistic reception, studying cultural policies and audiences in museums, cinemas, television, video, dance saloons, rock concerts; cultural tourism and urban heritage. She has given conferences and seminars in Mexico, Argentine, Brazil, Colombia, Venezuela, Spain, Portugal and Germany. She is part of Mexican and international research networks such as the Program of Urban Culture, the project México's Cultural Challenges Facing Globalization and the Brazilian-Portuguese Network of Urban Studies. She coordinated a Research Group on Cultural Consumption at Clacso (Consejo Latinoamericano de Ciencias Sociales), formed by specialists from six different Latin American countries. Her PhD thesis analyzes a century of cinemagoing in Mexico City, articulating the study of the audiences' ways of behavior within the theaters with the changes in the forms of use of urban space.

Evelyn SCHULZ is Professor of Japanese Studies at the Japan Center of the Ludwig-Maximilians-University in Munich. She obtained her Ph.D. at the University of Heidelberg and her *venia legendi* (*Habilitation*) from the University of Zurich, Switzerland. Specialized in modern Japanese literature and urban studies, she is especially interested in the relationship between urban space and text as well as discourses on modernity and the city, in particular Tokyo. She has published a comprehensive monograph concerning this field of research (*Reports about the Prosperity of Tokyo* (*Tōkyō hanjō ki*): *A Genre of Japan's Topographical Literature and Its Images of Tokyo*), 2004; in German). The focus of her most current studies lies on issues of urban revitalization, globalization versus localization, and re-evaluation of small urban spaces and their respective images, as revealed in the literature on Tokyo and other Japanese cities. In cooperation with Christoph Brumann (Max Planck Institute for Social Anthropology Halle, Germany) she is editing a conference volume on *Urban Spaces in Japan: Cultural and Social Perspectives* (Routledge, 2012).

Lidewij TUMMERS [l.c.tummers@tudelft.nl] graduated in 1989 as building engineer at TU Delft (NL); since 1999 architect and dwellers consultant at Tussen Ruimte, Rotterdam (www.tussen-ruimte.nl); between 2006-2010 Assistant professor at the chair of spatial planning and strategy, TU Delft; 2009-2010 Guest lecturer in *gender_archland*, the Forum for Gender Expertise at the Faculty of Architecture and Landscape Architecture, Leibniz University Hannover, Germany, funded by Maria Goeppert Mayer Grant; 2011-2012 Guest researcher at Maison des Sciences de l'Homme, funded by Le Studium Centre for Advanced Studies. Founding member of the *European Network of Experts on Gender, Diversity and Urban Sustainability GDUS* (www.rali.boku.ac.at/gdus.html) and board member of the *Dutch Organization for Renewable Energy ODE* (www.duurzameenergie.org).

Paul WALEY is a senior lecturer in Human Geography at the University of Leeds. His research grows out of a strong focus on specific geographic settings both in East Asia and Southeastern Europe. Tokyo has provided the context for much of his research, but he has also worked in Taipei and is currently involved in research projects in Belgrade and Trieste. Recent publications include Japanese Capitals in Historical Perspective: *Place, Power and Memory in Kyoto, Edo and Tokyo*, co-edited with Nicolas Fiévé (RoutledgeCurzon, 2003), *'Tokyo-as-world-city: reassessing the role of capital and the state in urban restructuring'* (*Urban Studies*, 2007, Vol. 44, No. 7), *'Distinctive patterns of industrial urbanization in modern Tokyo, c. 1880–1930'* (*Journal of Historical Geography*, 2009, Vol. 35, No. 3), and *'Introducing Trieste: A Cosmopolitan City?'* (*Social and Cultural Geography*, 2009, Vol. 10, No. 3).

Gordon WINDER is a geographer with interests in the historical experiences of globalization, imperialism, industrialization, urbanization, and environmental transformation. Born in New Zealand, he obtained his PhD at the University of Toronto, and worked at the University of Auckland, before moving to the LMU Munich in 2008 to develop his research interests at the intersection of economic geography and economic history. The main focus of his recent research is historical geographies of the news and news agency.

1. Spaces of Poverty, Spaces of Prosperity: Incomplete Tourist Encounters in Mexico

Eveline Dürr

1. Introduction

This article explores[1] a contentious kind of urban tourism in the city of Mazatlán, which is located at the Pacific coast of one of Mexico's northern states, Sinaloa. It is here where a multi-denominational church offers regular tours to the city's garbage dump as a tourist experience. Slum tourism has become an attractive activity worldwide and is tied into both the growing representation of the urban poor as well as the increasing mobility of tourists in the context of globalization. Critical voices focus on ethical issues regarding the commodification of the most vulnerable social groups and reject these activities as "poorism"; others stress the potential of tourism for the development of the local economy and the alleviation of poverty (Selinger & Outterson, 2009; Ashley, Roe & Goodwin, 2001). To this day, there is no clear answer to these controversial issues and empirical studies focusing on the concrete consequences of these activities are still scarce. It also needs to be understood that slum tours vary considerably in nature, style, scale, and intention. While some tours are primarily business-oriented, others are supporting local projects and define themselves as awareness-raising endeavors (Freire-Medeiros, 2008; Rolfes, 2009). Furthermore, regardless of their orientation, slum tours are strongly shaped by the specific urban condition in which they occur and the wider regional context.

In what follows, I scrutinize a non-profit slum tour in Mazatlán which is embedded in the philanthropic ideology of an evangelical church. In order to place this tour into perspective, I first discuss the ambivalent nature of tourism and its impact on the city of Mazatlán. I particularly stress the tourist industry's consequences regarding the urban spatial layout. I then explore the tour emphasizing the entanglement of spaces of poverty and prosperity, such as the garbage dump and the tourist district which are perceived as separate or even as dichotomous. While these spaces are appropriated, dominated, and controlled by different groups, they overlap, intersect, and depend on each other in particular ways. I wish to apply Foucault's idea of heterotopias as a conceptual approach of spaces which challenge, contest, and convert the normality of ordinary spaces and represent otherness and exceptionality (Foucault, 2008, see also Tonkiss, 2005, p. 30ff, 131ff; Dehaene & De Cauter, 2008). Furthermore, these spaces are especially differentiated and segregated in both physical and social terms. This is the case for both the tourist district as well as the garbage dump. Depending on the perspective, they can both be conceptualized as heterotopias. Their difference and otherness impedes full understanding and exploration which adds to their air of mystery (Genocchio, 1995). I argue that this characteristic makes the encounter between middle class tourists and dump workers incomplete and elusive. Nonetheless, tourism brings contrasting spaces into contact, transgresses boundaries, and creates new arenas of encounter.

2. Tourism's Ambivalent Character: Spatial Dimensions

In many countries of the Global South, tourism is on the increase and has become a key earner of foreign currency (Cleverdon & Kalisch, 2000, p. 172). Tourism however does not necessarily go along with economic prosperity, but rather has the potential to widen the gap between the rich and the poor and to aggravate social inequality. The negative effects of tourism, such as water shortages and pollution, gentrification, and the displacement of the local population, are well known and widely discussed. Critical voices explicitly point to the inequalities created by economic dependencies and try to bring consumers and producers in touch with each other (Cleverdon & Kalisch, 2000, p. 174). As a consequence, consumers have become more sensitive to these topics, increasingly demanding ethical standards (Cleverdon & Kalisch, 2000, p. 173; Urry, 1995). This critical tendency has given rise to tours with particular themes, such as social justice, ecology, or human rights, and to revised forms of tourism such as Fair Trade Tourism or Responsible Tourism. Other alternatives are framed as "niche tourism", offering meaningful experiences and sophisticated practices that differentiate this clientele from "mass tourism" (Novelli, 2005).

Tourist related service industries boost migration in many countries of the Global South and are linked to commuting as well as seasonal and short-term migration (Coles & Timothy, 2004, p. 3). While the tourist flow is usually from the countries of the Global North to the countries of the South, there is also a movement in the opposite direction, specifically of migrants from poor to rich countries. As Mowforth, Charlton, and Munt (2008, p. 5) point out, these flows might be very different in nature and duration of stay but they are still related as they are both linked to the economy. Both types of migration provide sources of income for the countries of the Global South, either in the form of remittances or as inward investment. Furthermore, a growing middle-class in the countries of the Global South produces national tourists, which again show different travel and habitual practices from international ones.

Cities and towns play a central role for tourists' movement and accommodation. Urban-based tourism holds a strong economic potential but also constitutes a threat to underprivileged citizens. More often than not, city authorities are eager to present a clean and safe environment, which catalyzes gentrification and often entails a ban on that kind of existing urban life which is referred to as the informal economy. But still, tourism is seen as a route out of poverty by powerful political and financial actors, such as the World Bank, which demands secure, clean, and healthy cities in order to promote tourism (Mowforth, Charlton & Munt, 2008, p. 178).

Today, tourism is a highly diversified activity and ranges from backpackers and mass tourism to first class travel arrangements. Regardless of the budget, travel experiences are ways of exploring new prospects and lifeworlds. Traveling is more than a movement through space as it is reflexive and entails an engagement with the familiar and unfamiliar, often blurring the boundaries between the native and the foreign, home and abroad (Rojek & Urry, 1997). Traveling as a spatial practice has a range of effects and can both reaffirm or unsettle confidence and

[1] This contribution is based on fieldwork conducted in 2009, including interviews and participant observation. For more details on this research refer to Dürr (n.d.).

identities as it may challenge conventional presumptions. What is more, travel and tourist experiences do not just impact upon those who are on the move but also strongly affect the host countries and respective local environment.

The city of Mazatlán is situated in this context and faces this very issue. Apart from a thriving fishing industry and one of Mexico's most important seaports, the city's economy rests on the tourist industry. White beaches, picturesque historic buildings, luxury golfing, and fishing facilities attract national and international visitors, predominantly from the USA and Canada. Tourism impacts immensely on the urban layout, streetscape, and built environment. The majority of the hotels and restaurants are located in the so called Golden Zone in the north of the city, which is connected to the historical center, itself located four miles to the south, by a scenic beachfront avenue. These major tourist districts are equipped with fast-food restaurants, souvenir shops, and other amenities catering to the tourists' needs. North of the Golden Zone is a marina with huge hotel resorts, condo complexes, private residences, and trailer parks. The construction of luxury hotel complexes is ongoing. The total population of Mazatlán is 438,434 (INEGI, 2010), with 1,861,658 visitors in 2008[2]. For most of their stay, the visitors linger in these particular spaces of the city. Tourists are also brought in for day trips by the cruise ships stopping in Mazatlán on their way along the Pacific coast. Street vendors move into the tourists' spaces to sell crafts and food at the beaches but can hardly be found in other spots of this manicured zone (Fig. 1). They live in the growing underprivileged districts at the periphery of Mazatlán, along with other migrants who find work in the tourist district during the high season.

Fig. 1: Vendors in tourist spaces at the beach front in Mazatlán, Mexico.
Photograph: © Eveline Dürr.

3. Spaces of Poverty, Spaces of Prosperity: Encounters at the Garbage Dump

It is in the midst of spaces of leisure and luxury where the Vineyard Ministry, called *La Viña*, is located. The Vineyard Christian Fellowship of Champaign, Illinois, is the home church of the Vineyard Church in Mazatlán. This evangelical church was initially born out of the hippie movement in California and has spread internationally (Watling, 2008). In Mazatlán, *La Viña* offers services in Spanish and English on a regular basis. The English service is attended by tourists but also by the local community of retirees from the USA and Canada, who are seeking a warmer climate during the cold northern winter months. The church runs a range of charitable projects in disadvantaged neighborhoods, such as mobile schools, feeding centers, and medical clinics. The most prominent project however is a guided tour to the city's garbage dump offered to tourists. Besides humanitarian efforts the tour provides an opportunity to advertise the church's missionary work. In this vein, the dump tour might be criticized for instrumentalizing the urban poor to raise funds and attract new converts (Fortney, 2007). Nonetheless, it is the church's ideology to keep social and missionary work apart in order to avoid criticism (Collom, 2004).

The half-day tour is run once a week during the low season from April to October and several times a week during the high season. It can be taken at no cost, but donations are encouraged. The tour is designed to challenge Mazatlán's shiny tourist image and purposely stresses antithetic urban spaces. The luxury resorts, the fancy cruise liners, the upmarket hotels, and condos along the marvelous beach front stand in stark contrast to the poor conditions of the garbage collectors, living in squalor and stench; these segregated spaces are meant to be brought together in the tour. In this vein, the tour is advertised as "the Other Mazatlán," as "an opportunity to visit the Mazatlán that tourists never see" (Hall, 2007, p. 63). The church's intention lies in the Christian faith-based understanding of charity but also in the aspiration to raise awareness for the poor, to act as an eye-opener, and to introduce the tourists to the "real" world (Weiner, 2008). Promising to lead into the "real" Mazatlán implies that there is an unreal, staged version of the city which is tailored to match the tourists' expectations but does not necessarily reflect the "authentic" city life. The dump tour provides an alternative to beach fronts, cultural heritage, and historic sites. It is a way into "authentic" but also alien spaces that are otherwise inaccessible to most middle-class tourists. Thus, the appeal of the tour goes far beyond the desire to see the "real" life of the city but is rather tied to the wish to experience the segregated and unknown. The heterotopian nature of the dump is accentuated by its geographical location as it is set apart from the tourists' everyday world, located at the urban fringe. Simultaneously, it is a racialized space of social periphery and marginalization where the bodies of dark-skinned garbage collectors, perceived as dirty, smelly, and unhealthy, contrast with the white, clean, and healthy ones. The dump is messy, dangerous, and extraordinary, thus suspending normality, order, and security. The tourists leave their protected spaces behind for the adventure of exploring the counter-image to their routine.

The US-American guides plays a key role in this expedition as a broker between antithetic

2 Secretaría de Turismo del Estado/Departamento de Enlace Tecnológico, 2008.

spaces and cultures. Their presence allows the tourists to safely enter a space which they are usually excluded from and would not feel comfortable to approach otherwise. This perception is enforced by the fact that the dump is a controlled and segregated space in tangible terms, closed off with a movable barrier and checked by the local police. Eerily reminiscent of the affluent gated communities in the city, entry is regulated by a gatekeeper. Accessing the dump is both a symbolic and concrete act of transgression, making spatial and social boundaries porous.

The guides' role as mediators is also stressed during the briefing before the tour actually starts. They provide a brief orientation on how to move in and into a disorderly space by explaining the protocol and the rules that apply when visiting this site, such as picture taking, greetings in Spanish language, and not handing out cash. They deliver some background information regarding the livelihood at the dump, such as the various stages of sorting and recycling the rubbish. Many tourists are keen to know more about the life at the dump[3] where the garbage collectors search for anything that can be recycled, sold, or otherwise used. The guides highlight their social exclusion, misery, and lifeworld, and portray them as people in need of both material and spiritual aid. These narratives help to assert difference by juxtaposing the ordinary and the extraordinary.

Fig. 2: Tourists interacting with garbage collectors at the dump in Mazatlán, Mexico.
Photograph © Eveline Dürr.

Finally, after a bus ride through some of the underprivileged neighborhoods, the tourists are placed in the midst of trash and squalor at the dump for around twenty minutes. Only the dump workers who have an interest in this encounter approach the bus, the ones who reject this activity do not come forward. Tourists are encouraged to interact with the garbage collectors by handing out bags with food and bottled water (Fig. 2). Often, both sides try to communicate with each other, each one trying to say some sentences in the language of the other, shaking hands, watching each other closely, or using sign language. It is a highly sensual encounter, getting close to foreign bodies' smell and sweat. But it is always an incomplete encounter, where the individuals catch a glimpse and a taste of the other but are not able to fully immerse in the other's heterotopian space, far less lifeworld. Exploring, participating in and understanding the other's space can only be elusive and tentative. Therefore, the mystique remains on either sides, even though the spatial and social barriers that usually separate spheres of poverty and prosperity are transgressed in the moment of encounter. But this should not hide the fact that even in this momentary encounter, power imbalances remain in place.

4. Conclusion

Tourism plays a pivotal role in creating particular urban spaces, economies, and social relationships. In Mazatlán, the urban layout is immensely shaped by the tourist industry. The tour to the garbage dump uses the enormous contrasts created by the tourist industry and portrays spaces of prosperity and poverty as counterparts. The attraction of the tour is both the sensation of the "other" and the "authentic" world as opposed to a compromised tourist version. It becomes an expedition in a heterotopian space which challenges the tourist perceptions of normality and security. These activities hold the potential to transform poverty districts from banned neighborhoods into spaces of contact and consumption. This process might help to raise the profile of poor neighborhoods and their dwellers in the context of the city and beyond but it involves their space being exploited as part of the lucrative tourist industry. There is the risk of converting misery, deprivation, and racialized social inequality into a theme-park-like experience, as is the case with other tours leading into poor districts or sites of catastrophes (Freire-Medeiros, 2009). Furthermore, the actual participation, agency, and opinion of the garbage collectors with regard to these tours are rarely articulated and need further investigation. This is crucial for a better understanding of their conditions, expectations, and needs and, in my opinion, for an adequate debate on ethical conduct and a more complete tourist encounter.

3 The tourists' motivations for participating in a slum tour are discussed elsewhere (see Dürr fc.).

References

Ashley, C., Roe, D., Goodwin, H. (2001) *Pro-Poor Tourism Strategies: Making Tourism Work for the Poor: A Review of Experience.* London: Overseas Development Institute.

Cleverdon, R. & Kalisch, A. (2000) 'Fair Trade in Tourism.' *International Journal of Tourism Research* 2: 171-187.

Coles, T. E. & Timothy, D. J. Eds. (2004) *Tourism, Diasporas and Space.* London: Routledge.

Collom, F. C. (2004) *The Dumb Gringo. How Not to Be One in Missions.* o.O., Xulon Press.

Dehaene, M. & De Cauter, L. (2008) *Heterotopica and the City. Public Space in a Postcivil Society.* New York: Routledge.

Dürr, E. (fc.) 'Urban Poverty, Spatial Representation and Mobility: Touring a Slum in Mexico', *International Journal of Urban and Regional Research*, Special Issue, (forthcoming).

Fortney, V. (2007) 'Loving Orphans Make His Heart Sing: Troupe Founder "the Gringo of the "Hood"', *Calgary Herald*: A9.

Freire-Medeiros, B. (2008) And the Favela Went Global: The Invention of a Trademark and a Tourist Destination, in: M. M. Valenca, E. Nel & W. Leimgruber (Eds.), *The Global Challenge and Marginalization*. (New York: Nova Science Publishers).

Freire-Medeiros, B. (2009) 'The Favela and Its Touristic Transits', *Geoforum* 40: 580-588.

Foucault, M. (2008) Of Other Spaces (1967), translated by Lieven De Cauter and Michiel Dehaene, in: L. De Cauter & M. Dehaene (Eds.), *Heterotopia and the City. Public Space in a Postcivil Society*. (London: Routledge).

Genocchio, B. (1995) 'Discourse, Discontinuity, Difference: The Question of "Other Spaces"', in: S. Watson & K. Gibson (Eds.), *Postmodern Cities and Spaces*. (Cambridge: Blackwell).

Hall, A. C. (2007) *Mazatlan IS Paradise.* New York: iUniverse, Inc.

Instituto Nacional de Estadística Geografía e Informática INEGI (2010) Censo de Población y Vivienda.

Mowforth, M., Charlton, C. & Munt, I. (2008) *Tourism and Responsibility. Perspectives from Latin America and the Caribbean.* London and New York: Routledge.

Novelli, M., Ed. (2005) *Niche Tourism. Contemporary Issues, Trends and Cases.* Amsterdam: Elsevier.

Rojek, C. & Urry, J. Eds. (1997) *Touring Cultures: Transformations of Travel and Theory.* London: Routledge.

Rolfes, M. (2009) 'Poverty Tourism: Theoretical Reflections and Empirical Findings Regarding an Extraordinary Form of Tourism', *Geojournal* DOI 10.1007/s10708-009-9311-8. Published online: 26 September 2009 http://www.springerlink.com/content/x6u6p46u22823453/

Selinger, E. & Outterson, K. (2009) 'The Ethics of Poverty Tourism', Boston University: School of Law Working Paper No. 09-29. http://papers.ssrn.com/sol3/papers.cfm?abstract_id=1413149#

Secretaría de Turismo del Estado/Departamento de Enlace Tecnológico (2008) *Mazatlán: Afluencia Turística según procedencia, 2004-2008.* (Mazatlán, Sin., Mexico: Secretaría de Turismo, Gobierno del Estado).

Tonkiss, F. (2005) *Space, the City and Social Theory.* Cambridge: Polity Press.

Urry, J. (1995) *Consuming Places.* London: Routledge.

Watling, M. (2008) *Natuerlich uebernatuerlich. Die Geschichte der Vineyard-Bewegung.* Witten: Brockhaus Verlag im SCM-Verlag.

Weiner, E. (2008) 'Slum Visits: Tourism or Voyeurism?' *New York Times - Travel*, 9 March 2008.

2. Creating Creative Cities?: Cultural Administration and Local Authorities in Japan since the 1970s

Mari Kobayashi

1. Introduction

During the past decade, structural administrative reform and the New Public Management policies in Japan have been implemented in a rapid and radical manner. In particular local governments have been profoundly affected by two policies enacted at the national level, namely (1) municipal amalgamation and (2) privatization. Before the year 2000, there were over 3000 local governments representing Japanese cities, towns, and villages. By 2009, however, the number had declined to about 1800 due to the policy of municipal amalgamation. After the revision of the Local Government Act in 2003, local governments could, at their own discretion, designate private companies and organizations to manage public facilities on terms usually limited to three to five years. This is known as the Designated Manager System and part of the policy of privatization. In contrast to the more gradual kind of privatization, which has been carried out in other countries in Asia as well as Europe, the Japanese case presents itself as a radical social experiment.

This fundamental shift in cultural policy originated in the Japanese economic affluence of the 1980s. The rise of corporate philanthropy and cultural patronage during this time had a great impact on the promotion of arts and culture. At the regional level, local governments built many opulent multipurpose theaters and concert halls, said to exceed 3000 in number throughout Japan. Many of these newly erected cultural facilities, however, have been criticized in the media for lacking the "software" of theatrical groups or orchestras (to perform in them) as well as management personnel trained in cultural administration (to operate them). In other words, many critics have pointed out the inherent contradiction of regional governments first financing the construction of such extravagant facilities but then being unwilling to cover operational expenses. This lamentable state of affairs has become even more conspicuous in the midst of the ongoing economic downturn that followed the bursting of the economic bubble in the early 1990s.

Below I will draw attention to some of the issues of cultural administration of local authorities that have arisen since the 1980s and examine the factors that have led to successful resolutions in some cases.

2. What is the Designated Manager System?

The Designated Manager System (*Shitei kanrisha seido* 指定管理者制度) is an administrative system introduced by new provisions in the Local Government Act, which was enacted in 1947 and has undergone a number of revisions since then. Based on the "principle of local autonomy" promulgated in Article 92 of the Japanese Constitution, the Local Government Act governs (1) the organization of local governments, (2) their relation to the central government, and (3) the establishment of administration at the local level with the purpose to be able to respond to the residents' needs. According to Article 10 of the Local Government Act, any person who resides in a given locality possesses the right to receive public service on an equal basis, in return for fulfilling his or her residential obligations. According to Article 244, the purpose of local government is to improve residential well-being and it is, therefore, responsible for installing "public facilities" to this end.

There are various kinds of public facilities administered by local governments, such as roads, public transportation and utilities, hospitals, parks, childcare facilities, kindergartens and schools, libraries, museums, public halls, community facilities, concert halls, theaters, and sport facilities, etc. Such facilities provide services to local residents. Sometimes local governments manage these public facilities directly but they may also entrust management to organizations that meet certain requirements. Typical examples include "municipal cultural promotion" and "municipal sports promotion" foundations established by local governments. These foundations are quasi-public corporations that represent the so-called "Third Sector."

In 2003, the Local Government Act was revised to lift limitations regarding who could be entrusted with the administration of public facilities. Local governments can now turn management over to legal entities that include for-profit private corporations as "designated managers." This change is part of the current trend toward deregulation and privatization promoted by the Japanese government. This legal revision does, however, not legally require privatization and, therefore, must be distinguished from the formal disposition of public facilities into private hands. The Local Government Act is a mechanism by which a designated manager executes a public service on behalf of the local government itself[1]. Under this system, a local government chooses the best supplier of a public service, which might be itself. Therefore, the first issue that automatically arises is whether or not a given local government is the best supplier of the public service in question. If not, the local government needs to select a designated manager.

The local assembly is responsible for this kind of designation and any related administrative matters. The basis on which such decisions are made depends on the particular local government. In the best case scenario, a given local government that designates a manager for a certain cultural facility will seek to (1) provide a detailed statement regarding the mission and purpose of the facility, (2) clarify the city's cultural policy, (3) concretely specify what the local government expects of the designated manager, (4) set guidelines and guarantees for what local government will pay for the service, and (5) establish a special committee of experts to oversee art, arts management, cultural policy, and general public policy, which will be responsible for making public presentations. In the worst-case scenario, the local government will make its decision based merely on trying to find the least expensive management option. While many local governments take the character of the facility into account, some do not. The latter prioritize cost-reduction over quality. In such cases, they select a building management and maintenance company which offers use of the facility to whomever wants to rent it. Only in big cities such as Tokyo does this not present a problem as professional arts companies like orchestras, drama, dance, and opera companies, etc. are concentrated there. Such arts companies indeed rely on borrowing public or private cultural facilities for staging performances.

---

1 Traditionally, the term "public" has referred to the bureaucracy, that is, to state ministries and local governments. "Public service" is thus supplied by the state, local government, or quasi-governmental bodies. Since the tragedy of the 1996 Hanshin Earthquake, which caused over 6000 deaths and large-scale suffering, public consciousness of the existence of non-profit voluntary activities has grown tremendously. In 1998, the Japanese government passed the "Act to Promote Activities by Non-Profit Organizations." Since then, there has been a shift in how Japanese people conceive of the "public," so that the term covers not only governmental bodies but also non-profit organizations and private companies. Of course, voluntary activities have a long history in Japan, but only recently have they come to be included within the meaning of "public."

3. The Concept of "Cultural Administration"

Why have local governments constructed so many arts facilities? To understand the social and economic factors originally involved one must go back to the 1970s. During this time some local governments recognized the importance of developing a cultural policy, which was initiated as Cultural Administration (*Bunka gyōsei* 文化行政). In 1972, the governor of Osaka Prefecture at that time set up the "Osaka Cultural Promotion Society" (Osaka Bunka Shinkōkai) which consisted of university researchers, writers, and so on. They discussed the distinctive characteristics of Osaka's culture (in comparison with Tokyo and other cities) and how these could be financially supported. They published their research as "Rethinking Cultural Life in Osaka" (Osaka no bunka wo kangaeru) and "The City and Its Culture" (Toshi to bunka). The contents of these policy reports show that there were various types of discussions held by the society. In "Osaka no bunka wo kangaeru" one can find discussions on what is special about Osaka's culture, the responsibilities of the city's administration to help promote and manage culture, international exchange, mass communication, urban regeneration and planning, regional development, and even environmental issues, to state only the most important topics.

Osaka Prefecture and Hyogo Prefecture each set up a Department of Culture (Bunka-ka) in their respective governments in the mid-1970s (nearby Kyoto Prefecture had already established one by 1966). Keiichi Matsushita, the political scientist who had taken the initiative for developing the concept of the cultural administration for local authorities, characterized the background of the situation as follows. Firstly, achieving sustained economic growth and widespread industrialization had led to an increased uniformity of Japanese society; it had become imperative that local governments review the quality-of-life issues keeping in mind the distinctive characteristics of local regions. Secondly, he stressed the need for local authorities to create autonomous and decentralized political systems to take full advantage of these regional characteristics[2]. Hence, the purpose of the cultural administration of local authorities according to Matsushita was to encourage the formulation of policies based on each region's distinctive history and cultural requirements. There were no special laws for cultural promotion or cultural development; the local authority only needed to provide a political rationale to carry out projects initiated by Cultural Administration. Matsushita and Mori Kei were strong advocates of the principle of the Cultural Administration[3].

They pointed out that the principle of the Cultural Administration consists of three parts. First of all, the regional culture belongs to the residents of that area, which means the distinctive personality of the regional culture is shaped by those who live there. Local authorities should never interfere with the local culture to alter it; they can only support it (the principle of "local residents' autonomy"). Secondly, the praxis of cultural administration should be exercised by municipality or, alternatively, the lowest level of local authority close to the area in question (the principle of "municipality initiative"). Thirdly, the public administration should not simply perpetuate the established cultural administration but rather implement innovative approaches (adhering to the principle of "administrative innovation").

Comparing with existing cultural administrative affairs, one can find some central points of this principle of Cultural Administration. Firstly, up to that point, cultural activities were mainly linked to personal and individual behavior, overseen by the educational administration, and considered as adult education. Most local authorities built libraries and museums as a possible chance for citizens to learn, but compared with the overall educational expenditures the funding was meager and the whole approach was rather laissez-faire. The target of Cultural Administration is regional culture and identity. Secondly, by introducing and stressing the municipality's initiative new attention was brought to various regional cultures in Japan. Thirdly, Matsushita made clear that citizens' activities were necessarily on the forefront of finding and creating regional culture. He brought forth the notion of a citizenship which was responsible for its own regional culture and the promotion thereof. In the 1960s, citizens were considered to be fundamentally antagonistic to the government and local authority. Matsushita defined the "citizens" as the subjects that needed to seek, promote, and improve the quality of life in and culture of their region. Fourthly, in order to realize this goal local governments had to reform their behavior, regarded citizens' participation as vital, and, therefore, support the citizens. Fifthly, the label Cultural Administration (*Bunka gyōsei*) was a deliberate effort to avoid the use of the totalitarian-sounding "Cultural Policy" (*Bunka seisaku* 文化政策). Matsushita noted that the term "Cultural Policy" invoked memories of the totalitarian cultural policies of the 1930s and the wartime period, when propaganda promoted nationalistic causes.

Let us then consider what concrete accomplishments the Cultural Administration has achieved at the municipal level. Matsushita and Mori introduced various case studies in their "Cultural Administration: Self-innovation of Local Authority" ("Bunka gyōsei: Gyōsei no jikōkakushin"). For instance, city planning incorporating parks and sculptures, city planning for children, city promotion with a fairy-tale museum for everyday use, urban design, 1% system for culture, and so on.

It is also important to mention that around this time, Umesao Tadashi played an instrumental role in the implementing of cultural administration in Osaka Prefecture. Umesao was formerly an anthropological researcher in Kyoto University who later became the director of the National Museum of Ethnology. He wrote "Introduction to Cultural Economics: The Economic Value of Cultural Facilities" ("Bunka keizaigaku kotohajime - bunkashisetsu no keizai kōka"). He advocated that local authorities must build cultural facilities to make culture flow naturally, like water from a faucet. In the 1980s, local authorities began to construct cultural facilities under directives from the new Cultural Administration policies. The idea that cultural facilities must flourish in the region had become prevalent among the local authorities.

2 The Japanese constitution regulates the autonomy of local authority. But the reality was and still is somewhat different from the law. The power and financial control of the central government and its Ministries have always been strong. It has only been in the 1990s that the General Act for the Decentralization was enacted.

3 Mori Kei was a professor at Hokkaido University after he had been administrator of the Department of Culture in Kanagawa Prefecture. He was specialized in matters regarding the autonomous administration of local authority.

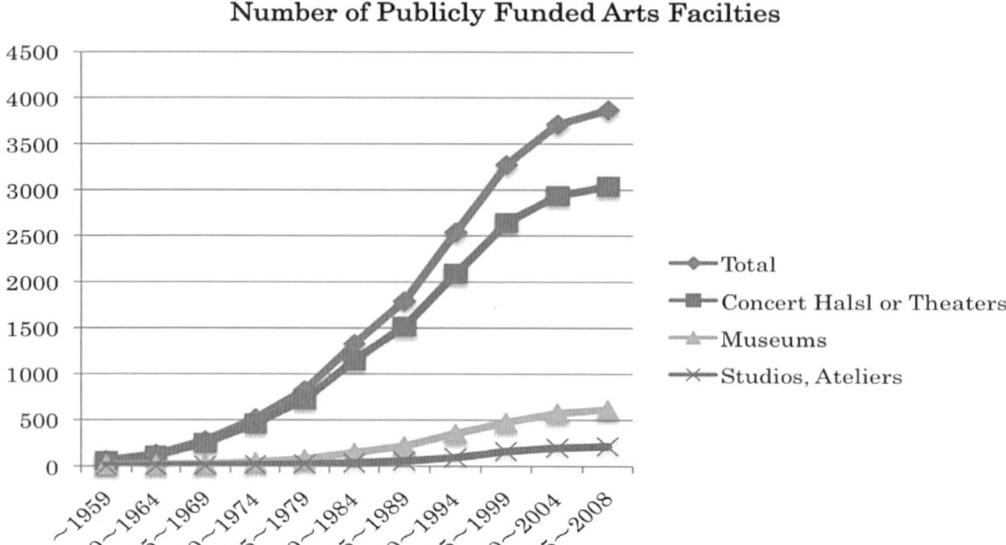

Number of Publicly Funded Arts Facilities

4. The Problems of Publicly Funded Arts Facilities

This chart shows that the number of municipal cultural facilities has rapidly increased from the 1980s onward[4]. Until 1990, the central government did not oversee the construction of regional arts facilities since it did not possess a general arts policy for Japan and the Agency for Cultural Affairs didn't exist yet[5]. There is no national legislation regarding theaters and concert halls, which are only briefly mentioned in the Fire Defense Law. Instead, local government ordinances provide the goals for and regulation of such facilities. For instance, legislation regarding a "City Arts Center" will specify the purpose of this facility, but generally only in very vague terms like "to promote regional culture or arts."

The general situation is described as follows in a report entitled "Investigation by the Research Committee on the Activities of Public Cultural Facilities" prepared by the Agency for Cultural Affairs. "There are 2,031 theaters and public cultural centers throughout the country as of May 2000[6]." Many of these facilities are underutilized. According to the committee, "active steps toward maximizing the use of public cultural facilities can be accomplished by (1) studying the regional specialties and character of the facilities and taking a lead in flexible management, (2) strengthening the central role played by a regional culture for the region and its residents and supporting the function of the facilities in question in promoting art culture, and (3) upgrading management capabilities."

Moreover, a report prepared in 2000 by the Japan Foundation for Regional Art Activities entitled "An Investigation of Foundation Management in Regional Cultural Facilities," offered the following advice. A foundation should (1) reflect its present circumstances and environment, (2) reflect its mission, (3) take the lead in revitalizing its management in response to brain drain and organizational reforms, (4) make the most of a given facility's functions, (5) direct new energy into addressing its problems, which are essentially problems of cultural administration, and (6) respond to the needs of local residents. These prescriptions outline the issues faced by regional publicly funded arts facilities. This is the background of the implementation of the Designated Manager System.

5. Conclusion:

To conclude I pose the question of whether local authorities have actually been able to create "creative cities" under the new policies of the Cultural Administration. The concept of Cultural Administration was designed with the aim of fostering cultural creativity in cities or regions in an innovative manner. In practice, cultural facilities were constructed but new policies of Cultural Administration were not implemented. New facilities were built all over Japan but they were managed in the old bureaucratic ways. The widespread construction of these cultural facilities without "software" were recognized as problematic. At the same time, the government promoted the privatization of public facilities by introducing the Designated Manager System, which was designed to help alleviate management and financing problems.

General concerns regarding simple privatization soon became apparent. As I mentioned above, the worst-case scenario is that cost-reduction is valued higher than the quality of programs and facilities. Moreover, the entry of new companies into competition for running publicly funded facilities has resulted in some arts foundations being dissolved after losing out, their staff facing unemployment. As the "Designated Manager" contracts for most arts facilities run from three to five years the full impact from the introduction of this new system has yet to be seen. For instance, as far as stage technology maintenance is concerned, the easiest way to bring down costs is to hire non-regular employees with little experience or retirees. Many questions arise concerning whether or not it will be possible to ensure safety and functionality even after the contracts run out. Moreover, years of preparation are needed to stage big international exhibitions and performances or for inviting well-known artists and performers. Will Designated Managers, with relatively short-term contracts, be willing to take on the challenge and commitment of such long-term planning? The potential long-term impact must be studied carefully.

On the other hand, the Designated Manager System has also exerted some positive influence. Firstly, some local governments that take the promotion of culture in their region seriously have shown greater initiative in developing their own cultural policies. They situate the physical arts facilities within the context of such cultural policy to realize their overall goals. From the 1980s onward, local governments have put greater energy into creating a vision as well as legislation and planning to promote culture. However, in a number of cases, their ambitious plans were not sufficiently thought through to allow the effective execution of policy. More conscientious local governments have carefully reviewed and revised their long-term plans, while others have come up with entirely new proposals.

Secondly, one might say that the slimming down of bureaucratic management has allowed foundations to better recognize and consolidate their core missions.

4 This chart is from the "Investigation Concerning Public Cultural Facilities in the Region" conducted by the Japan Foundation for Regional Art Activities in 2008. This foundation was established by the Ministry of Public Management, Home Affairs, Postal Services, and Telecommunications.

5 The Agency for Cultural Affairs is an external bureau for the Ministry of Education, Culture, Sports, Science, and Technology.

6 In Japan, there are two major national bodies that keep track of the number of publicly funded cultural facilities, namely the Association of Public Theaters and Halls in Japan and the Japan Foundation for Regional Art Activities. Since there are various types of facilities in Japan, the overall numbers differ in accordance to how the organization defines specific cultural facilities.

Thirdly, and this is related to the first point, renewed attention is paid to the best ways to utilize cultural facilities. As mentioned earlier, given that facilities such as cultural halls and museums are institutions imported from the West, it is worth discussing whether or not Western styles of management should be employed. The optimum means of utilizing cultural facilities will differ in accordance with region and scale. The recent shifts in state and local policy, however, have given us a good opportunity to re-visit such critical issues.

I will briefly point out that there are indeed some notable success cases. For instance, in a small city in Kochi Prefecture, a non-profit organization was founded by citizens to preserve knowledge about the distinctive cultural heritage of the region, and they now manage a publicly-funded museum called Ekin-gura. Another successful example is the small but well-designed theater "Za Koenji" (The [Theatre] Koenji) established by the Suginami ward of Tokyo, which is managed by a non-profit organization supported by the Japan Theater Association (Nihon Gekidan Kyogikai). This arts facility is operated and utilized by personnel that have special expertise in theater management. These are just two of many successful instances of implementing new concepts and policies of Cultural Administration. There are also numerous cases of local authorities trying to establish cultural promotion ordinances or creating cultural promotion plans that are sustained by the creative and enthusiastic input of local residents. In all these cases though it is crucial to acknowledge that local residents have provided both the impetus and means for creating the creative city.

References

Matsushita Kei'ichi and Mori Kei (ed.), "Bunka gyōsei: Gyōsei no jikō kakushin," 1980, Gakuyō shobō.

Umesao Tadao (ed.), "Bunkakeizaigaku kotohajime: Bunka shisetsu no keizai kōka," 1988, Gakuyō shobō.

3. Projects of Creativity and Inclusion: The Challenges of Cultural Development in Mexico City

Ana Rosas Mantecón

1. Introduction

The *Creative City* model has been applied in cities all over the world. At the same time that it has been praised for its successes, which have been widely promoted by Richard Florida, this model has also been questioned because of its propensity to generate gentrification as well as segregation. For example, Carles Guerra has pointed out how in Barcelona improving land value has become more important than human living conditions (Carles Guerra, 2007:152). Similar conclusions have also been reached by Andrew Ross (2003) in the case of New York City and by George Yúdice (2008) in Miami; the latter of these two cities has been catapulted to the status of a "global city" based on its thriving fashion, entertainment, and communications industry. Despite the commonly employed rhetoric concerning diversity, Miami has been unable to overcome the existing sharp class as well as racial tensions.

In view of these contradictions, an alternative *Creative City* model has been implemented in European cities, like Dublin, Belfast, or London, and some Latin American ones such as México City, Medellin, and Bogotá. It has proven efficient in improving social interaction, reverting deterioration of public spaces, and fighting violence and crime. This is an example of how cultural development as the cornerstone for restructuring social tissue, fighting crime, improving living standards, transforming values, and creating a bridge for dialogue between different sectors of society can produce great benefits. This paper analyzes three of Mexico City's projects (one by the city government and the others rooted in civil society) that work with marginalized groups of people in urban, conflicted areas. They appealed to cultural access and creativity as means to confront exclusion, violence, and debilitated social ties. **ConArte** (With-Art), **Cultural Territories for Equality**, and the **Faros Network** are all projects that exemplify good practices in the pursuit of cultural development. All of them have acknowledged the importance of promoting creativity to achieve urban regeneration, while they simultaneously have articulated the need to interweave politics of inclusion with those looking to regenerate social tissue and develop environments for interaction and sociability. As has also been recognized by UNESCO and UNCTAD, projects modeled in this way understand that we must turn to culture and creativity if we wish to invent new ways of facing the challenges of the globalized world.

2. The Creativity Challenge in Mexico City

When the twentieth century arrived, Mexico City was just a small town, covering no more than roughly 30 square kilometers total. Over the course of a few decades though, starting approximately in the year 1930, the city experienced an unprecedented acceleration in territorial expansion and population growth as a consequence of industrialization and the funneling of money in the form of investments into the Metropolitan Area. Mexico City's economic, cultural, and political dynamism also attracted large migratory flows that were a decisive factor for further acceleration of the population growth. At that time the City was conceived as a space of inclusion and modernity, full of employment and housing opportunities, political participation, and urban life. In other words, the industry and trade boom set the stage for a massive amount of newly created jobs, which in turn led to simultaneous urban development.

Beginning in the 1980s, the reduction of the fiscal budget limited the expansion of public infrastructure while urban growth continually increased. Due to the fact that accelerated urban growth was not the product of careful planning, it was also not accompanied by a decentralized expansion even of basic services. As a result, the vast majority of the population began to reside far from the city's south and center, where the majority of services were (and still are) concentrated, making access difficult. Especially the most recently urbanized municipalities show a notable lack of all cultural infrastructure, with the exception of cinemas and libraries. Yet it is not only distance that separates cultural infrastructure from its potential users. Other barriers that are closely related to chaotic urban development are the frequent occurrences of traffic congestion, violence, informal commerce in the streets, and city inhabitants favoring other leisure activities, like television and radio. This has promoted the disconnection of traditional spaces of interaction and has increased social and spatial segregation.

In addition to what has been stated before, the economic crisis that characterized the last quarter of the 20th century, resulting from the replacement of the import substitution model and the imbalance created by the new liberal economic model, was further intensified by the migration from an urban concentrated area to a multicentric metropolitan zone, unequal and segregated, with an increasing informal economy, unemployment, poverty, crime, and a decreased regulatory role of the state. The fragmentation and sheer dimension of the urban area (more than 1,500 square kilometers) has now made interaction between its parts impractical and has evaporated the physical image of its totality, whose scattered parts are only reconnected by the media.

Yet the challenges the city faces may also be viewed as opportunities to revitalize citizen organization. When nation-states lose the capacity to summon and administer the public sphere, cities resurge as strategic environments of "practicable citizenship", productive arenas to advance new forms of participation with more concrete and manageable references than may be the case under the logic of the "national" and "global" abstracts. What escapes the citizens' exercise in these fields may be recovered, to a certain extent, at the local level, which tends to be the place of residence, work, and consumption (Holston and Appadurai, 1996: 187).

Territorios de Cultura para la Equidad (Territories for Cultural Equality) is a *postfeminist* civil initiative that, since 2005, has been working with women suffering from *constrained citizenship*, that is, women who have been excluded from the benefits of macroeconomic development, the arts, and artistic expression. This civil initiative has prioritized strategies of recognition, exercise, and defense of the right to culture and the recreation and enjoyment of the arts through projects that open spaces to access cultural offers, encouraging creativity through body language, music, and writing workshops, and making encounters between participants enjoyable in the joint search for inclusion, personal, and social revaluing, as well as in search for recognition and respect for individual differences. They have developed various projects with female citizens from different walks of life, such as retired sex workers, young students, non-profit activists, police officers, and city street sweepers. Later, work done at the workshops has been shown in temporary exhibitions at different museums, in published books, and through performing arts.

ConArte. *Consorcio Internacional Arte y Escuela* (WithArt. The International Consortium of Art and School) is a civil society organization that, along with other public and private (national and international) institutions, seeks to promote art education in public schools, in order to develop creative, expressive, and self-recognizing capacities within children and young people. The project conceives art as a fundamental resource for the comprehensive education of all people, not only of those who aspire to become artists. It seeks to contribute to equality and shorten the gap that separates the school from contemporary cultural transformations by fighting the new aesthetic illiteracy, giving children and adolescents new capacities for appreciating culture, and widening their communicative and expressive abilities through artistic language. Through a joined effort with the Public Education Ministry, **ConArte** (WithArt) has started different programs like "Learn to Dance", implemented in primary and middle schools in Mexico's Historical City Centre. Using an innovative concept, it teaches dance to children, working on the basis of making movement and music tangible and understandable. Instead of a particular type of dance, the program seeks to develop movement abilities, music appreciation, participation, and individual as well as collective evolvement with respect to different capacities. Weekly classes take place for grades four through six and the first year of middle school (the grade with the highest dropout rate, coinciding with the age some adolescents begin delinquent activity). With the support from the **National Dance Institute of New York,** teachers are continuously trained by **ConArte** in specialized artistic languages and pedagogical methods, enriched by school environments, urban culture, and Mexican tradition.

The **Faros de Artes y Oficios** (Network of Arts and Guilds Factories), a public art and community project, was initiated after the inauguration of the first autonomous government in Mexico City[1]. Recognizing that inequities manifest in the concentration of cultural infrastructure, as is the case in artistic and cultural formation, the **Partido de la Revolución Democrática** (Party of the Democratic Revolution) sought to improve the territorial distribution by investing in existing infrastructure and to create new audiences. The first **Faro** was built in Iztapalapa, one of Mexico City's most populated, conflicted, and poorest municipalities (where 20% of migrants reside) with a notoriously deficient cultural infrastructure. The area serves as the gateway for drugs into the city, which are trafficked by armed gangs. The **Faro** was constructed in what was once an abandoned warehouse and has since then served as a neutral area between marked gang territories. In subsequent years, four more **Faros** were built in similarly poor, conflicted areas with limited or no access to the city's cultural infrastructure.

The **Faro** model was conceived as a three-dimensional approach. It is a project of urban development through the formation of public cultural centralities. It is also a project of artistic and labor education through guild and artistic workshops. Finally, it is a project of **cultural offering** (with permanent programming services and spaces such as galleries, libraries, playgrounds, documentation centers, computer rooms with internet access, scenic spaces, book clubs, etc.). The action model is based on the principle of the union between arts and crafts as two elements that are woven into one activity, that is, the development of art through learning a craft to further promote creativity. Through teaching a trade (such as carpentry, lighting design, iron work, the use of sign language or of new technologies, set and costume design, handmade paper production, glass blowing, hydroponics, horticulture, etc.) and providing art workshops (theater, music, literature, dance, painting, photography, sculpture) it helps attendants to acquire skills, recognition, and financial reward. It also seeks to encourage dialogue with the artistic community as a whole through internships and community service experiences. The impact of **Faros** is far-reaching; artistic work enriches community parades and festivals, contributes to the formation of cultural activity leadership, and legitimizes culturally marginal productions, such as museum exhibits on urban graffiti displaying art produced at the workshops.

3. Conclusion

These initiatives are broadening the notion of what the *creative class* is due to the fact that they are geared not only towards artists and are in tune with the international assumption of a necessity to have cultural politics occupy a central place in the political world. This perspective has led to remarkable changes in the mechanisms by which cultural politics are defined. Not only professional artists are now being considered as key agents of politics but also non-professionals and community members.

One of the greatest difficulties that this inclusive creative city model faces in Latin America is having been instituted at a time of emergency, either due to the failure of security programs or because of the militarization of public spaces. This has tended to favor a purely instrumental use of creativity, undermining its experimental form, and assigning expectations that cannot possibly be fulfilled when using the model in an isolated way. The biggest challenge is continuity, because these cultural projects only yield results at the medium to long term. Such continuity tends to be fragile, depending on a constant search for resources and negotiation opportunities with a wide array of institutions. In the cases that I have analyzed, dependency on various sources of public financing has made their operative autonomy fragile and their programmatic proposals hard to accomplish. The projects analyzed in this paper are in favor of building new cultural participants as part of a permanent process, over the course of many years. Political logic on the other hand favors more spectacular cultural events, which tend to have a larger audience without the same structural impact, as in the case of the **Nomadic Museum** that, in 2008, managed to attract a total of 8 million visitors at the City Centre's main square in three and a half months. Furthermore, they also encourage acknowledgment and defense of cultural rights, contradicting traditional government practices used to seek legitimacy through conces-

1 In 1997, the Mayor of Mexico City was democratically elected for the first time. Before then, he had simply been designated by the president. In 2000, the Municipal Public Officials (*Delegados*) were elected democratically for the first time.

sions and mere giving (promoting co-optation and control through selective access to resources or bombastic cultural offers). **Territorios de Cultura para la Equidad, ConArte**, and **Faros de Artes y Oficios** are examples of *good practices* that link creativity with interaction, reconnect the fragmented city, as well as help construct citizenship. They are intended to impede the conversion of our cities into areas solely dominated by the free market forces. They seek to counteract the decline of public space in its role as a place for interaction and for learning to respect diversity. In the end, efforts need to be joined so that we may still practice urbanity as defined by Jerome Monnet, not only as peaceful recognition of others but as "the art of living together with the city as our mediator".

References

Florida, R. (2002) *The Rise of the Creative Class*, New York: Basic Books.

Holston, J. and A. Appadurai (1996) Cities and Citizenship, *Public Culture*; 8(2), 187-204.

Guerra, C. (2007) Das Macba – Ein unter Widrigkeiten entstandenes Museum / Macba, un museo formado en la adversidad", in: Charles Esche y Barbara Steiner (eds.), *Mögliche Museen*, Walter Koening Buchverlag, Koln, pp. 147-158.

Landry, Ch. et al. (1996) *The Art of Regeneration: Urban Renewal through Cultural Activity*. Stroud: Comedia.

Monnet, J. (1997) Espacio público, comercio y urbanidad en Francia, México y Estados Unidos, *Alteridades* (Universidad Autónoma Metropolitana-Iztapalapa), 6(11), 11-25.

Ross, A. (2003) *No-Collar: The Humane Workplace and Its Hidden Costs*, Philadelphia: Temple University Press.

UNESCO (1996) *Nuestra diversidad creativa*, París: UNESCO.

UNCTAD (2008) *Creative Economy Report. The Challenge of Assessing the Creative Economy: Towards Informed Policy Making*, http://ssc.undp.org/creative_economy.

Yúdice, G. (2008) Modelos de desarrollo cultural urbano: ¿gentrificación o urbanismo social?, *Alteridades* (Universidad Autónoma Metropolitana-Iztapalapa), 18 (36), 47-61.

4. Revitalizing Tokyo's Back Alleys as Areas of Cultural Sustainability and a Decelerated Lifestyle

Evelyn Schulz

1. Introduction

It was a decision of great historic significance when Tokyo was designated to be Japan's capital in 1868, during a time when the country was striving towards a modernization based on Western models. Since then Tokyo has undergone far-reaching transformations regarding its political, economic, social, and cultural systems. Tokyo has been regarded as the most important showcase of Japan's modernity and had to be designed correspondingly in order to promote this image. During the last century the city has been reconstructed into a "ceremonial center" (Fujitani 1996) of the nation and has become an important tool for shaping memory and nostalgia as well as evoking visions of the future. Accordingly, many architectural landmarks can be found in Tokyo, each representing visions of modernity as they existed at a particular period of time.

It is no exaggeration to claim that Tokyo has recently been one of the most contested spaces in Japan. The city is a major battleground for various, in many cases directly opposing, visions of modernity and is regarded both to be at the cutting edge of Japan's future as well as a space that preserves certain aspects of the past. In other words, Tokyo is associated with two different Japans, the premodern and the modern Japan, Japan as a global player and Japan as a proponent of local traditional cultures. It is in this city where, more than in any other city, Japanese modernity and its respective images have been staged and restaged, represented and contested. The more Tokyo has been modernized and redesigned the more traditional patterns of urban space have been erased. As it is true that Tokyo's old downtown residential and business districts suffered from a lack of sanitation, from overpopulation and diseases, as well as from a high risk of fire there were indeed many good reasons to attempt to improve living conditions by tearing down the old quarters. It is understandable that they were considered to hinder progress and modernity. Plainly put, living there was regarded as inconvenient, outdated, and even dangerous.

However, today, this tendency seems to have come to an end, at least in certain areas of Tokyo. In recent years, the so-called *roji*, basically narrow alleyways and backstreets that had fallen out of grace almost completely during the 20th century, are gaining more and more attention.

The word *roji* 路地 denotes a loosely defined pattern of urban space. It implies a set of particular urban structures, streetscapes and vernacular architecture and relates to specific forms of everyday lifestyles and neighborhood relationships. *Roji* are small-scale and low-rise mixed-use areas in residential neighborhoods promoting local commercial activity. *Roji* form a maze-like network of narrow lanes and side streets that in many cases are just wide enough for a single person to either walk or cycle through. Very often they are also dead-end streets.

These areas function as pockets of social values and local cultures; they provide an intimate atmosphere. Neighborhood life is organized along the lane with its small shops and res-

Picture 1: *roji* in Kyoto, with a shrine at the end of the alleyway

taurants, often owned by local people. It is in these cramped areas that Japan's urban dwellers grew accustomed to greeting, talking, and arguing with one another. In recent years, there has been a growing interest in revitalizing a number of Tokyo's remaining *roji* instead of knocking them down. The participants of such activities are residents and local citizens' action groups as well as architects, writers, and artists.

The purpose of my paper is to show how the *roji* on the one hand have been erased during the 20th century while on the other hand they simultaneously evolved as a spatial concept opposed to Western ideas of urban planning. Furthermore, I intend to illustrate how this kind of resistance and counterculture has contributed to the diversity of urban space in present-day Tokyo and how the *roji* are re-evaluated as assets essential for a prosperous urban life as well as for Tokyo's long-term goal of improved attractiveness and livability.

2. Transforming Tokyo into a Global Megacity: The Erasure of Small-Scale Residential Quarters and the Revival of "Slow City" Zones

Most of Tokyo's architectural landmarks and transport routes are the product of a political and economic agenda that attempted to transform the inner city of Tokyo along the guidelines of Western urban planning theory. This resulted in the construction of new institutions and wide open streets, the introduction of public transportation systems as well as sewers and water works to improve public hygiene. Later on, the promotion of private motorized transport had a great impact on Tokyo's urban fabric and the way people used to live. All of these as well as many other innovations steadily led Tokyo to loose its original structure, namely that of a "city on water". As a consequence traditional lifestyles, too, disappeared over time.

Edo, the name of Tokyo until 1868, had previously been called a "city on water" (*mizu no toshi*) (Jinnai 1993 and Jinnai 1995:66–118). Tokyo's infrastructure and transport system were based on an extensive network of moats, canals, and rivers which connected the densely populated merchant and craftsmen quarters, which in turn were often located along Edo's waterways.

Picture 2: Keelboats (*yakatabune*) floating on the Edogawa in present-day Tokyo

Catastrophes such as the Great Kantō Earthquake of 1923 and Tokyo's destruction during the war years of 1944 and 1945 but also the building boom of the 1980s (*bubble economy*) as well as Tokyo's rise to the status of a global city in the last decades have accelerated the transformation of Tokyo's cityscape and urban fabric (Sorensen 2002). Since the 1960s, many *roji* areas have been replaced with office buildings and multistory condominiums, both allowing a more effective land use.

Rising land and housing prices have accelerated the elimination of *roji* areas further. Many of the remaining *roji* areas are targets for urban development projects. During the last ten years the trend of moving "back to the city centre" (*toshin kaiki*) initiated a boom of inner-city redevelopments not only in Tokyo but also in other Japanese cities. In many inner-city neighborhoods comprised of small two to four story dwellings high-rise residential buildings, so called *manshon*, of 20 to 50 stories are being built. Since 2000, the number of such residential towers has increased drastically (Hirayama 2003). The recovery of residential functions in the core area of Tokyo goes hand in hand with the construction of large mega-structures such as Shiodome, Roppongi Hills, and Midtown Tokyo, all of which have accelerated the transforma-

Picture 3: Tokyo's cityscape

tion of Tokyo's cityscape from low-rise to high-rise.

Such massive integrated high-rise property developments attempt to be cities in themselves. They include residential areas, shopping malls, office and administrative buildings, amusement and leisure areas. They are regarded a key element to Japan's competitiveness in the future and are meant to emphasize Tokyo's position as global city. In contrast to these integrated high-rise property developments *roji* are de-monumentalized space patterns that cater to the need to scale down the city to human scale and to create pedestrian zones for slowing down the pace of urban life.

Urban researcher Hisashige Tetsunosuke lists five conditions for a decelerated urban way of life in his book on urban development theory titled *The Japanese Slow City: Community Building that Revives the Particular Culture of the Region and Its Natural Environment (Nihon-ban surō shiti. Chiiki koyū no bunka, fūdo o ikasu machizukuri*; 2008:32):

1) Humanism: People can walk around in people-friendly public spaces at a comfortable pace.
2) Slow food: People can enjoy locally produced food.
3) Involvement: Citizens can participate in the region's culture and folklore.
4) Exchange: People can talk to each other, look at the scenery, and are comforted by being in the space.
5) Sustainability: The lifestyles and intentions of the citizens are taken into consideration.

Urban spaces that do meet these five conditions are the *roji*. From the point of view of the opponents of monumental urbanism the *roji* areas have become to function as counter-spaces to Tokyo's globalized areas. According to urban researcher Darko Radovic they promote socially and culturally sustainable environments. In this respect, the *roji* denote not only a particular pattern of urban space rooted in Japan's premodern culture but also represent a spatial concept which includes criticism of mainstream modernity as well as resistance to the capitalization of urban space. (Radovic 2008).

3. Indigenous Concepts of Urban Environments: The *Roji* as Manifested "Decelerated Other" Modern Urban Space

Both, the achievements of 20th century modernity as well as its negative aspects and the corresponding cultural, political, and poetic ramifications have been reflected in the way space and manners have been depicted in literary works and films set in Tokyo. In general, here the *roji* are associated with the "other" in a positive sense. They are regarded as small-scale spaces, which preserve authentic and local everyday life culture. However, it is recognized that although they are located outside the realm of Western style urban modernity *roji* are nonetheless deeply affected by it. For example, the film directors Ozu Yasujirō (1903–1963) and Naruse Mikio (1905–1969) produced many movies in which they converted the *roji* into a stage for the discourse on the pros and cons of modern urban family and social life (Satō Tadao 2002:17–34 and 47–72).

The starting point for this discourse on the *roji* and what they stand for can be traced back to literary works published in the first decade of the 20th century. In particular the works of the well-known writer Nagai Kafū (1879–1959) are regarded as important media for keeping the memory of the culture and lifestyle of the *roji* alive. Kafū has been called Tokyo's chronicler. He has become famous for his lifelong habit of daily walks through Tokyo and of writing about his experiences. Issues of spatial dynamics in general and the Edo-Tokyo transformation in particular form the underlying context of most of his writings (Schulz 1997). In many of his works the narrator strolls through Tokyo, acting as a critical spectator of modernity; instead of praising the new Tokyo, he laments the loss of the past. A representative example of Kafū's way of depicting Tokyo is *Hiyorigeta* (*Fairweather Clogs* or *Wooden Clogs for Good Weather*), a collection of essays about strolls through Tokyo, published in 1914. Similar to a guidebook, *Hiyorigeta* offers a simultaneous approach to both the spatial as well as the temporal aspects of urban space in Tokyo. But instead of introducing the reader to new landmarks of the time such as the parliament, train stations, and steel bridges, Kafū had a keen eye for those traditional patterns of urban space that were disregarded by the modernization policies of the state government.

Hiyorigeta starts with reflections about the advantages of exploring the city by foot in order to have a look at those places where people actually live (Nagai, 1992–95, Vol. 11:111–112). In this respect the chapter about *roji* is especially revealing. According to Kafū, in the Edo period the vitality of the city largely originated from the teeming back alleys, which were lined with shops, small houses, restaurants, and brothels. Kafū perceives the *roji* as enclosed spaces, which are separated from Tokyo's modernity in both geographical as well as cultural terms. He created a pattern of depiction of the *roji*, which alternates between realistic depiction and nostalgic rhetoric. Kafū praises the shadowy and hidden atmosphere of the *roji*. In contrast to the main streets lined with Western-style shops the twilight of the *roji* produces an atmosphere of sadness and truly human feelings. The *roji* are calm and quiet locations relieving stress and pressure. In short, while the *roji*, generally speaking, are home to the less fortunate they nonetheless offer various forms of living and life-styles (Nagai, 1992–95, Vol. 11:152–153).

Hiyorigeta has become a canonical text of Tokyo walking literature and a model for similar accounts of Tokyo. Not only writers refer to Kafū when writing about Tokyo though. Ordinary people interested in the history of Tokyo also follow in his footsteps. Motivated by a renewed interest in Kafū's intense relationship with Tokyo *Hiyorigeta* has become a stimulating text for exploring Tokyo's *roji* areas.

4. Diversifying *Rojiron* (Discourse on *Roji*) in Contemporary Japan

Since I started my research on *roji*, roughly five years ago, countless literary walking guides have been published for Tokyo. This indicates that the exploration of Tokyo on the basis of literary works is an important method for getting access to its history. This is due to the fact that many *roji* areas are infused with a kind of *genius loci* of the history and culture of Edo-Tokyo. Moreover, during the last five years the concept of *roji* has, or rather the concepts of *roji* have, diversified tremendously. Classically, the *roji* are seen as spatial arrangements that point to an urbanity that cannot be grasped with terms grounded in Western theory. In this respect, the notion of the *roji* fills an epistemological gap and expresses a need for plural concepts of urban space. Recent publications about *roji* can at least be divided into four groups.

4.1 *Roji* as Part of the Discourse on Architecture and Urban Planning: Building Sustainability

During his lifetime, Kurokawa Kishō was one of the leading architects of Japan. His works and writings are characterized by an intense examination of both Western as well as Japanese principles of architecture and urban planning in order to overcome dualistic thinking and to incorporate other cultures in his works. In one of his later publications, *The Revolution of City* (*Toshi no kakumei*, 2006), Kurokawa claims that the revitalization of the *roji* is the key to the future of Japan's cities. Thus, Kurokawa stresses the value of the discarded, seemingly unimportant spaces that have rarely been recognized as significant in conventional urban discourse (Kurokawa 2006:86).

However, the situation seems to have changed to a certain extend. In January 2010, a group of architects published *The Design of the Revitalization of Roji Quarters: Learning from Roji the Art of Revitalizing Living Spaces* (*Machi roji saisei no dezain: Roji ni manabu seikatsu kūkan no saiseijutsu*; Usugi, Aoki, Iseki et al. 2010). This comprehensive volume provides an overview of the formation and development of *roji* areas in the urban history of Japan and refers to many non-Japanese examples of similar urban structures, such as for instance the old towns of Pamplona and San Sebastian in Spain and of Xi'an in China. Numerous examples of existing *roji* are carefully analyzed regarding their modernization and revitalization potential.

4.2 Mapping and Documenting the *Roji*

The starting point for the process of mapping and documenting of Tokyo's *roji* can be seen in the activities of the architectural historian Jinnai Hidenobu. From the 1980s onwards, his strong interest in Tokyo's topographical and historical layers turned him to walking through Tokyo in order to trace its underlying structures. He elaborates on the results of his research in his study titled *Reading Tokyo's Quarters: Reading the Historical Living Environment of Shitaya and Negishi* (*Tōkyō no machi o yomu: Shitaya, Negishi no rekishiteki seikatsu kankyō o yomu*, 1981). Shitaya and Negishi are both located near Ueno area and are very well-known *roji* areas. Both are said to have preserved the atmosphere of traditional urban dwellings while simultaneously offering the commodities and conveniences of modern urban life.

It seems that Jinnai's approach has laid the basis for the growing interest in the mapping of Tokyo's *roji* areas. The architectural historian Okamoto Satoshi, who studied under Jinnai, wrote a comprehensive study about the past and present of Tokyo's well-known *roji* areas by the title of *The Roji of Edo Tokyo: Discovering the Attraction of Places on the Basis of a New Sensibility* (*Edo Tōkyō no roji: Shintai kankaku de saguru ba no miryoku*, 2006). In contrast to these works, which focus on Tokyo's core area, the urban planner Tateno Mitsuhiko published an atlas of Tokyo's *roji* areas in which he documents both, those *roji* in Tokyo's core area as well as those which are hidden in the suburbs (Tateno 2005).

Picture books such as *Hundred Backstreets of Japan* (*Nihon no rojiura 100*, 2005) and the succeeding volume *New Hundred Backstreets of Japan* (*Shin Nihon no rojiura*, 2008) as well as *Roji: Wandering Back Alleys* contain numerous photographs of *roji* from all over Japan thus illustrating that *roji* are not limited to Tokyo (Satō Hideaki 2005 and 2008; Nakazato 2004). In contrast to these positive back-alleys Satō Hideaki also depicts empty and cluttered abandoned spaces between buildings and has designated them as *roji*. In a sense, a *roji* can even be a wasteland (Satō Hideaki 2005:110–111). *Tokyo Plus Walking Guide* (*Machi aruki gaido Tōkyō purasu*, 2008), finally, aims to guide locals as well as tourists to attractive and charming, multifunctional neighborhoods (TEKU.TEKU 2008).

4.3 *Roji* as Spaces that Preserve Memories and the Material Culture of the Past

In recent years, stimulated by a renewed interest in Kafū's relationship with Tokyo and in particular in *Hiyorigeta*, it has become popular walking practice to draw on Edo period maps, the so-called *Edo kiriezu*, in order to explore Tokyo's *roji* areas. Publications such as *Leisure Kiriezu Walks Through Greater Edo* (*Ō-Edo burari kiriezu sanpo*) and *Walking Edo Tokyo Using Kiriezu and Present-Day Maps* (*Kiriezu: Gendaizu de aruku Edo Tōkyō sanpo*) have in common that they guide the reader to spaces of everyday life, in particular those small-scale areas and alleyways that are still untouched by urban development projects (Nawata 1995 and Jinbunsha henshūbu 2002).

Another way of approaching the *roji* is to regard them as spaces that preserve memories. The picture book *Memories of the Roji* (*Roji no kioku*, 2008) nostalgically uncovers the reminders of the past and resonating memories still to be found in these back-alleys (Aku and Satō, (2008). *The Grand Exhibition of the Shōwa Period* (*Shōwa rojiura dai hakurankai*, 2001) locates pre- and post-war innovations in material culture in *roji* areas (Ichihashi 2001).

4.4 Real *Roji* Walking, Dwelling, and Shopping

Tokyo's remaining *roji* areas have withstood the destruction of war as well as a whole host of new developments. Since the 1980s, attempts are being made to maintain the mixed urban ecology of particular *roji* by revitalizing them in various ways. In most cases citizen communities have mobilized themselves with great determination and motivation to create a more sustainable and livable inner-city environment (Fujii, Okata, and Sorensen 2007). These areas are very successful not only in fostering strong neighborhood relationships but also in producing a fresh image of themselves or even gaining a status that can be called a brand, thus strengthening their local economies and culture. In doing so, they manage quite well to resist being overtaken by developers and to protect themselves from unwanted change.

Tokyo's most famous *roji* areas of this kind are Kagurazaka (神楽坂), Kichijōji (吉祥寺),

Picture 4: Tsukudajima represents the contractions between low-rise *roji* areas and high rise mansions

Tsukudajima (佃島), Yanesen (谷根千) and Shimokitazawa (下北沢). The name *Yanesen* refers to the three neighborhoods of Yanaka (谷中 , Ya), Nezu (根津 , Ne), and Sendagi (千駄木 , Sen). Each of these areas has its own local history and has successfully evolved a particular identity over time. Kagurazaka has become famous for its high-class restaurants. Kichijōji is regarded as a model for a new sustainable life-style and as a place where the creative, such as designers or writers, prefer to live and work (Miura and Watari Kazuyoshi Kenkyūshitsu 2007). However, due to its success rents are going up fast. Tsukudajima has become famous for its preservation of a local neighborhood with the Sumiyoshi shrine as its center and high-rise buildings in the background. At weekends, Yanesen's pedestrian walkways are flooded with people who are on leisurely strolls or shopping. Interestingly, the name Yanesen originates from a local journal of the same title that reports on local history, people, restaurants, and products. Shimokitazawa is known as an epicenter of youth culture and is said to be one of Tokyo's most culturally vibrant neighborhoods. In recent years, Ōkubo has become a trendy *roji* area and is regarded as a successful model for a multicultural low-rise mixed-use area in Tokyo. Due to its comparatively high percentage of foreign residents (nearly 10%, in 2003, many of them from East Asian countries) Ōkubo has to provide a culturally vital and dynamic urban environment that satisfies various lifestyles and consumer habits and needs (Inaba 2008).

However, the very success of such areas in establishing unique environments for both residents as well as visitors does not mean they are entirely immune from the danger posted by redevelopment projects. Recently, Shimokitazawa citizen groups have had to rally against large-scale development plans that would include the construction of department stores and a 26 meter wide road. This case shows that the preservation and revitalization of *roji* areas is always a process of negotiations from the bottom to the top.

5. Conclusion

The revival and revitalization of the *roji* addresses a variety of highly interesting aspects and issues, such as the need for Sustainability in urban planning, the current state and future of Japan's urban population, and the status of local culture in a global city, to name a few. Furthermore, the discourse on the *roji* is paralleled by a rising interest in the revitalization of Tokyo's waterways and waterfronts. Both types of urban space are in the focus of development projects which aim to create a network of pedestrian and recreational zones, not only for children and elderly people but also for the average urban citizen. Traditionally, Tokyo's *roji* areas were tightly connected with its waterways. The renewed interest in Tokyo's waterways again mirrors the trend to rediscover Tokyo's original topography and to make it accessible for its residents and visitors. The central aim is to make Tokyo more livable and greener. Against this backdrop, the notion of the *roji* is associated with a new vision of urban modernity which stands in opposition to modernist conceptions of city. The *roji* represent the informal, unplanned city that first formed and then matured due to the various activities of its residents.

However, one has to wait and see to which extent this vision will stand the test of time.

In the end, the discourse on the revitalization of *roji* areas at least sheds light on the important role of residential communities in creating more sustainable and livable environments on the one hand as well as the conflicts that invariably arise between the various parties that are involved in the negotiations connected to the processes already mentioned on the other. Recent publications such as *The Turning Point towards a Japanese Way of Building Cities* (*Nihongata machizukuri no tenkan*, 2007), a book that analyzes *roji* areas all over Japan and their potential to revitalize the city, seem to imply that the focus is purely and simply on indigenous Japanese urban spaces.

In any event, one has to keep in mind that here, too, the notion of *roji* as an alternative space and as a vessel for multiple histories and cultures only came into being in connection with modernist Western style urban planning. Starting with Nagai Kafū the rediscovery of the *roji* and their revitalization is set within the framework of visions of modernity that aim at a better future. Even if the notion of the *roji* presupposes a dualistic relationship such as Japanese space versus Western space one has to be aware that such dualisms often are less clear-cut than one might presume at first glance. The modern concept of *roji* could only have evolved through the interaction with Western concepts of urban space and, therefore, can't help but be entangled with Western ideas of modernity.

Furthermore, the discourse on the *roji* is deeply interconnected with that on mega-projects such as Roppongi Hills and Midtown Tokyo. Both of these discourses point to two central themes in the urban landscape transformation of the 21st century, namely the combination and promotion of both built heritage and innovative design of space. While the first represents the traditional urban design with rather local spatial references the second represents that of innovation with conscious universal, respectively global, spatial references.

However, both ways of urban design refer to each other, and even if it seems that one urban form is privileged over the other, in the end, that one, too, could not be without its counterpart.

References

Aku Yū and Satō Hideaki (2008) *Roji no kioku*, Tokyo: Shōgakukan.

Aoki Hitoshi (2007) *Nihongata machizukuri no tenkan: mini kodate saigairo no fukken*, Kyōto: Gakugei shuppansha.

Fujitani Takashi (1996) *Splendid monarchy: Power and Pageantry in Modern Japan*, Berkeley: University of California Press.

Fujii Sayaka, Okata Junichiro and André Sorensen (2007) Inner-city redevelopment in Tokyo: conflicts over urban places, planning governances, and neighborhoods, Sorensen, André, and Carolin Funck. *Living cities in Japan: citizens' movement, machizukuri, and local environments*, London et al.: Routledge, pp. 247–266.

Hirayama Yosuke (2003) Home-ownership in an unstable world: the case of Japan. Forrest, Ray and James Lee. *Housing and Social Change: East-West Perspectives*, London et al.: Routledge, pp. 140-161.

Hisashige Tetsunosuke (2008) *Nihon-ban surō shiti: chiiki koyū no bunka, fūdo o ikasu machizukuri*. Tokyo: Gakuyō shobō.

Ichihashi Yoshinori (2001) *Shōwa rojiura dai hakurankai*, Tokyo: Kawade shobō shinsha.

Inaba Yoshiko (2008) *Ōkubo – toshi no miryoku: tabunka kūkan no dainamizumu*, Tokyo: Gakugei shuppansha.

Jinbunsha henshūbu (2002) *Kiriezu: Gendaizu de aruku Edo Tōkyō sanpo*, Tokyo: Jinbunsha.

Jinnai Hidenobu, ed. (1981) *Tōkyō no machi o yomu: Shitaya, Negishi no rekishiteki seikatsu kankyō o yomu*, Tokyo: Sagami shobō.

Jinnai Hidenobu (ed.) (1993) *Mizu no Tōkyō*, Tōkyō: Iwanami shoten (*Bijuaru bukku Edo Tōkyō*, Vol. 5).

Jinnai Hidenobu (1995) *Tōkyō: A Spatial Anthropology*, Berkeley et al.: University of California Press.

Kurokawa Kishō (2006) *Toshi kakumei: kōyū kara kyōyū e*, Tokyo: Chūō kōron shinsha.

Miura Atsushi and Watari Kazuyoshi Kenkyūshitsu (2007) *Kichijōji sutairu: tanoshii machi no 50 no himitsu*, Tokyo: Bungei Shunju.

Nagai Kafū (1992–1995) *Kafū zenshū*, Vol. 11, Tokyo: Iwanami shoten, pp. 109-189.

Nakazato Katsuhito (2004) *Roji: wandering back alleys*, Tokyo: Seiryū shuppan.

Nawata Kazuo (1995) *Ō-Edo burari kiriezu sanpo: jidai shōsetsu o aruku*, Tokyo: PHP kenkyūjo.

Radovic, Darko (2008) *Another Tokyo: places and practices of urban resistance*, Tokyo: cSUR, University of Tokyo, ichii Studio.

Satō Hideaki (2005) *Nihon no rojiura 100 [hyaku]*, Tokyo: PIE BOOKS.

Satō Hideaki (2008) *Shin Nihon no rojiura*, Tokyo: PIE BOOKS.

Satō Tadao (2002) *Eiga no naka no Tōkyō*, Tokyo: Heibonsha.

Schulz, Evelyn (1997) *Tagebuch eines Heimgekehrten: Der Entwurf ästhetischer Gegenwelten als Kritik an der Modernisierung Japans*, Münster: Lit-Verlag.

Sorensen, André (2002) *The making of urban Japan: cities and planning from Edo to the twenty-first century*, London and New York: Routledge.

Tateno Mitsuhiko (2005) *"Edo – Shōwa" no rekishi ga wakaru Tōkyō sanpo chizu*, Tokyo: Kōdansha.

TEKU.TEKU (ed.) (2008) *Machi aruki gaido Tōkyō plus*, Tokyo: Gakugei shuppansha.

Usugi Kazuo, Aoki Hitoshi, Iseki Kazurō et al. (2010) *Machi roji saisei no dezain: Roji ni manabu seikatsu kūkan no saiseijutsu*, Tokyo: Shōkokusha.

All photographs @Evelyn Schulz.

5. Creativity Starts Here: Rotterdam (NL): Creative Citizens Meet Creative City Policies

Lidewij Tummers

1. Introduction

This paper was written on invitation during a guest lectureship at Gender Archland, LUH. It provided an opportunity to reflect on 20 years of practice amongst self-organized as well as institutional creative clusters in Rotterdam. Written from this subjective perspective, it does in no way claim to be thoroughly academic; the 'creative city' is not central to my research activities. Rather it is an attempt to place developments as seen from the perspective of the 'subjects of creative city policies' in a wider framework and to document the experiences made in the field. Each of the chosen cases represents a number of similar initiatives, each with a comparable yet unique configuration of participants and context, each more or less durable and successful in their attempts. As such, this documentation concerns itself with the *lived* creative city in order to give substance to theories that otherwise are just abstract concepts, in an emancipatory way.

The paper cannot do justice to the manifold initiatives in Rotterdam, let alone elsewhere. However it might help those who attempt to build the necessary bridges in understanding the gap between policies and creative production.

I would like to thank the organizers of the 'Creating Cities' conference for providing this opportunity and its contributors for the open and inspiring discussions. They certainly helped to further my understanding of the dynamics at work and the position of creative citizens in urban planning systems worldwide. My apologies go out to the creative citizens themselves for the simplifications that were necessary in order to keep the descriptions of the cases concise. I hope though that they will be the ones that benefit the most from the ongoing debate and that they will never give up.

2. Introducing Rotterdam

Rotterdam is the main port of the Netherlands. It is located in the southern part of the Dutch conurbation of Randstad, the most densely populated western area of the Netherlands (NL). Rotterdam City has about 600.000 inhabitants, the wider agglomeration almost 1.5 million (2009). It is statistically the poorest as well as the youngest city of the Netherlands, and in many schools the majority of students has both a Dutch passport as well as parents of foreign origin. In other words, the future of Rotterdam is a blend of different ethnicities and cultures.

Thinking about the Netherlands, Amsterdam is usually the city which springs to mind with its long-standing reputation for creativity. By contrast, Rotterdam is an important motor of the Dutch economy and until the 1980s was a city of workers with a low cultural profile. Until recently, Rotterdam was a shrinking city, losing especially young families to the nearby suburbs built in the 1980s and 90s.

A number of policies have been developed in an attempt to attract the middle class. Examples include terrace housing development, new public spaces, (minimum) income requirements in order to be legible to move into certain areas, and finally also to enhance the 'creative' or cultural profile of the city, referring to the ideas of Richard Florida.

While the growth of the 'creative economy' in Amsterdam (as well as Utrecht) is stagnating, Rotterdam has the space to accommodate this growing sector and has especially been attracting young cultural entrepreneurs and innovative artists over the past decade.

About 25 years ago, the change began with a program entailing considerable investments into the cultural sector, which was ultimately symbolized by the Municipal Councils' decision for the design of a new bridge as an architectural icon. The Erasmus bridge was opened in 1996 and has indeed become a new icon of the city. A number of parallel projects, such as NAI, Kop van Zuid with its skyscrapers, and the new theater have contributed to Rotterdam's current reputation as a city of architecture.

3. The Creative City Policy of Rotterdam

In 2005, the local authorities approved 'Rotterdam Economische Visie 2020' (Vision for the Economy of Rotterdam 2020) by the Economic Development Board Rotterdam (EDBR) and the Development Agency Rotterdam (OBR) and mapped in the 'Stadsvisie' (Vision for the City 2030)[see picture 1].

The Executive Programme 2006-2009 of the Economy Vision nominated three spearheads, namely the industry and port cluster, a medical cluster, and a creative cluster. Clearly, creativity is seen by Rotterdam authorities in economic terms; the policy documents refer to the 'creative economy' and instead of being embedded in the Cultural department's activities it is the responsibility of the OBR, the executive body for the real estate and land tenure ship affairs of the local authorities.

For Rotterdam the creative cluster was estimated to account for 3.3% of the general employment, which equals more than 10,000 jobs. Its 'value' is estimated at approximately €400M or an estimated 2.2% of added value to the urban economy.

According to the *Atlas voor gemeenten* (Atlas for Dutch Municipalities edition 2007) the Rotterdam creative sector in the wider definition grew by 33% between 1996-2004, which makes it the 10th fastest growing in the country. In the narrow definition, the growth is even faster with 43%, which makes it the 8th fastest growing nationally.

OBR located 40% of Creative employment in the city centre, indicated by the polymorf line on the map [Picture 1]. The light spots indicate the consumption of creative output such as theatres, galleries, shops; dark dots are established & OBR locations. As will shown later many, more dispersed, clusters of creative entrepreneurs do not appear on this map.

OBR focuses its creative policy on *facilitating and stimulating* entrepreneurship and crossovers. It has defined the following development factors:
    1. Stimulating creative entrepreneurship
    2. Accommodation for creative companies

3. Connecting creative companies with each other and the industry in general

4. A flourishing creative sector with a recognizable culture and events policy

5. A solid knowledge infrastructure regarding the field of creative economy

This paper addresses item 2, the accommodation that artists and creative producers need.

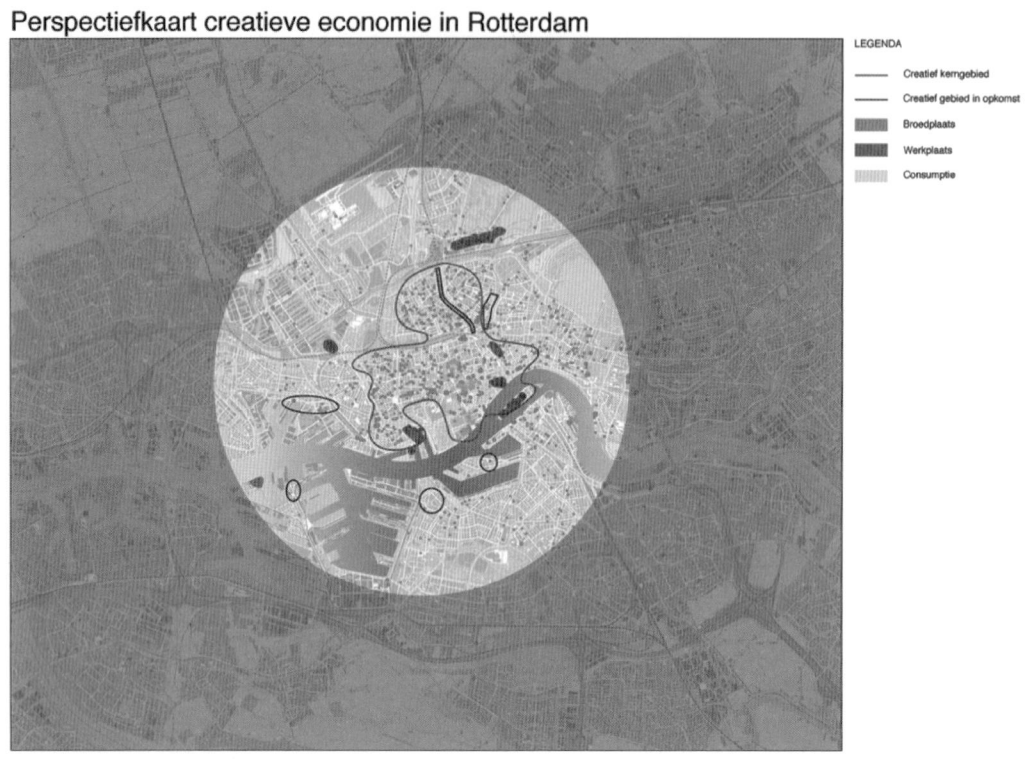

Picture 1: OBR map of Creative Rotterdam, Source: Economic vision, p16

4. Selected Projects of the City

Van Nelle: Architecture Factory

One of the first projects was the 'van Nelle Fabriek' (a former coffee and tobacco factory). The development of re-use started in 2000 after a long start-up period before the creative city policy really managed to take off. The factory is a monument to early modernist architecture, therefore its (re-) use is subject to strict regulations, regarding the exterior as well as the interior, the offices. The quality of the building lead to the central theme of 'architecture factory' and many architecture firms are housed here, as well as consulting engineers, and project developers.

Profile: 55.000 m^2 total, >100 units (av. 400m2), printing & copying facilities, restaurant, & conference rooms (on commercial basis)

rent: €95/m2/year, (min 40m2 /unit) including heating and security, excl. VAT

Schiecentrale: Film Industry

Another project Rotterdam is proud of is the former energy plant 'Schiecentrale' located at Mullerpier, a riverside area with other buildings attracting architectural tourism. Between 1997 and 2007, its large hall was converted into a film studio, at times doubling as performance room where other events (e.g. concerts) take place. The hall is surrounded by four floors of individual units, which are connected through a gallery/staircase and are occupied by professionals of the film industry, from editors to casting bureaus.

Profile: 1.700 m2 film/TV recording studio, local radio company, restaurant, conference rooms, 46 small units,

rent: €115/m2/year + additional costs + VAT

The Creative Factory

This former flour-processing plant located at Waalhaven (a port on the south bank of the river) opened its doors in 2008 for young start-ups, offering accommodation as well as intense side programs. Participants do not rent rooms but workplaces. They receive personal coaching. The creative sector aimed for in this project is geared towards graphic design, publicity, and other commercially viable forms of creativity. However, this concept is not suitable for creative entrepreneurs who rely on precious equipment such as musical instruments; insurance companies do not accept the arrangement.

Profile: total ±2.800m2 , 10 units with 160m² with 9 workplaces; €195-220 per place/month ex. VAT including WiFi, security, and reception; 2 units with flex spaces (part-time occupied/double rental) 7th floor 800m² for three large firms & Vestia Skylobby

5. Self-organized Creative Clusters in Rotterdam

A common feature of self-initiated clusters is the emphasis on artistic as well as financial autonomy. Their, often experimental, work tends to aspire to be self-financed rather than being subsidy oriented. Moreover, in Rotterdam, many 'crossovers' can be seen, such as collaborations of different ethnicities and between (artistic) disciplines. In a spatial sense, this means a combination of individual studios, meeting places, and spaces for performance as well as for socializing. For individual members it involves combining employment (e.g. teaching or a job at a museum) with autonomous projects.

For the creative production, a parallel economy exists for catering, technical support, transport, and so on. Many members are at the forefront of high-tech developments, as a means of expression or to maintain (digital) international networks. For some this is a permanent and desired lifestyle, for other a steppingstone to the life of an established artist.

As can be seen from this map from 2008[see picture 2], the self-initiated creative clusters are dispersed all over Rotterdam, in small pockets each with its specific history. There are so many of them that the smaller ones are not even listed. Which of the self-sustained initiatives are included at all in OBR statistics is unclear.

While the OBR seeks creatives, the creative producers look for accommodations. How does this work in practice? Are their intrinsic spatial needs met by the urban policies? What determines the relations between 'creatives' and 'officials'? Before going into these questions, a few cases of self-initiated clusters will be given.

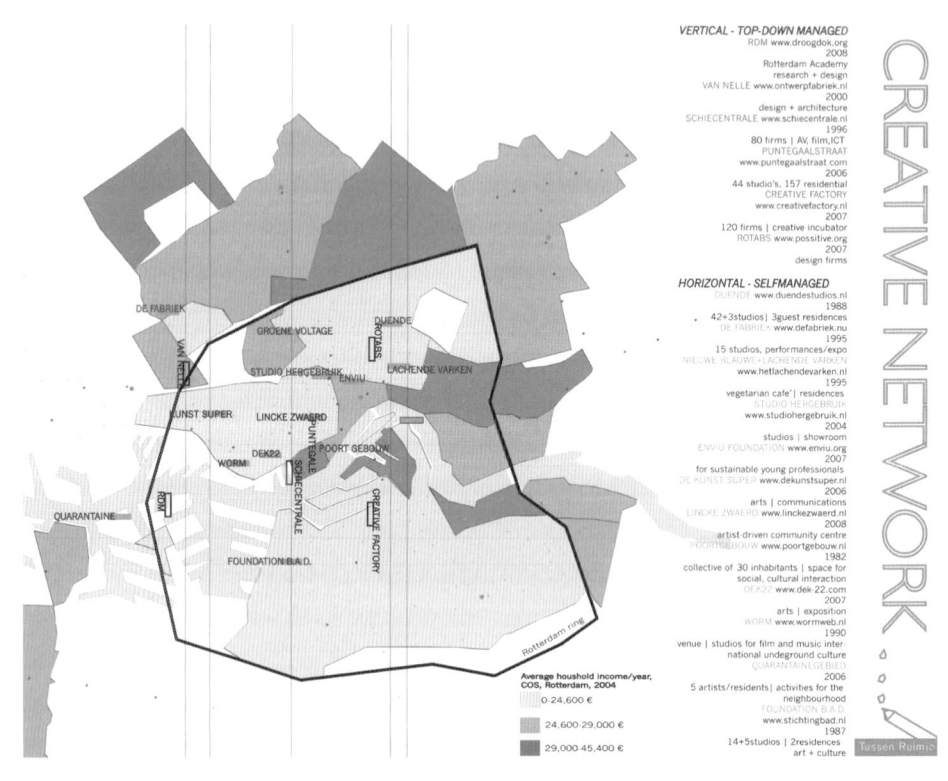

Picture 2: Mapping creative clusters in Rotterdam [Anna Romani, Tussen Ruimte, 2008]

6. Selected Self-organized Creative Clusters
POORTGEBOUW

The Poortgebouw may be the oldest creative cluster (in the contemporary sense) in Rotterdam. It was created in 1983 after an initial squat initiative in 1979, which lead to a process of negotiation and legalization. With the help of supportive professionals and public servants the building was converted into 30 units with shared facilities. The accommodation is equipped for the cohabitation of creatives; musicians can practice their instruments for example without disturbing the neighbors, there is room to give lessons, organize workshops with shared equipment that individual residents cannot afford, and so on. For the performing arts, such situations are generally hard to find. It is possible to organize performances and cook-ins although the size of the audience is restricted by fire-regulations. Poortgebouw is also an example of a monumental building rescued by spontaneous occupation in a period when it was empty, neglected, and threatened to be demolished due to the political spirit of the time. It survived largely through the effort of its creative residents.

Profile: 30 living+studio units ±25m2 each with shared facilities, band rehearsal room, kitchen/café, workshops, course room, etc. €275/month/unit rent incl. additional costs

WORM

Another initiative in Rotterdam is called WORM, which has also been established during the 1990s and which has a history of changing locations. WORM advertises as being 'an institute for avantgarde recreation, hybrid and hyperfunctional, for performers as well as audiences blending work, learning and entertainment' (from: *recreate*, WORM brochure 2010). It features a professional stage, a CD/music shop, and an audio-visual media studio, and is part of a worldwide network of experimental cross-over artists. After a 2-year period of negotiation and uncertainty, WORM is now (2010), with the help of the OBR, being transferred to the former building of the Photo-Institute, which in turn has been relocated to Wilhelminapier as part of a prestigious urban development project aiming to convince the upper middle class to settle in Rotterdam. This case demonstrates the chain of 'space for creativity' that is necessary, forming the steppingstones for individuals as well as the economy. A €1,600,000 rehousing fund is involved, far more than the annual staging budget.

Profile: recording studios, music shop, stage/concert hall for 200 pers., cinema/projection room for 40 pers., foyer for 100 pers., band rehearsal room, kitchen/café, workshops, course room, etc.

LINCKE ZWAERD

While WORM is a high profile project with international ambition Lincke Zwaerd offers a case of a different nature. Residents of an inner city street, most of whom are professional or amateur artists, were confronted in 2004 first with demolition and then with renovation of their homes to be rented as luxury apartments. They mobilized successfully to defend their rights as tenants. Picking up on the street's name *Zwaerdecroonstraat* the residents association Lincke Zwaerd, 'Agitated Sword', aims to create local meeting places, to organize street festivals reaching out across ethnicities, and to revive the local economy by the power of self-employed artisans and collective activities. The first step was to open garden fences and become acquainted with each other's studios and activities. This lead to a chore group installing a community center in an empty apartment. Although Rotterdam generally welcomes initiatives for 'social coherence' Lincke Zwaerd had to negotiate very hard for a guarantee to keep access to a community room after renovations.

Profile: ±150 dwellings+volunteers from the neighborhood maintain common garden, meeting room, cook-in and other activities.

DE FABRIEK

DE FABRIEK

'The Factory' is a dynamic group of people that are as varied as 'Taji the artistic chef', modern dancers, VJ's and webdesigners, graffity artists and painters, theater producers, and furniture makers. In 2006, they formed an association to share living space, offer affordable studios, share technology, organize public events, and do joined projects of art. The association's name is derived from their original location, a former factory (in Dutch: 'fabriek') that had been empty for decades. In winter of 2008, the health and safety department of the municipality performed an inspection and left an urgent (three days to comply) eviction notice due to fire risks. In spring of 2009, the artists brought their case before the local authorities. They referred to the Creative City policy, which had been put into effect in the meantime, claiming a position as creative producers and asking for mediation of OBR to obtain new accommodations. Instead, city hall sent another inspection team, which closed down the temporary accommodation immediately because of the (obviously) bad conditions. Currently, De Fabriek is housed at the edge of the city in a former paint factory, where redevelopment plans of the owner have been delayed due to stagnation in the real estate market. Residential and public functions are prohibited.

Profile: Originally: 6 living units ±25m2 with shared facilities, studio, band rehearsal room, kitchen/café, workshops, projection room with 49 seats, etc.

After first eviction: 35 artists sharing studios, dance rehearsal room, and carpentry workshop, meeting room with basic kitchen. Public events are suppressed.

After second eviction: 18 artists sharing 12 studios, shared kitchen, and living room. Public events are held in collaboration with other venues. €55/year/m2 rent. plus heating; €15 person/month membership for internet, management, PR etc.

7. Where Citizens Meet Creativity

The Lincke Zwaerd cluster is one example of how some 'creative producers' operate based on a set of autonomous values, how they create cross-cultural social networks, are involved in squatter or grassroots movements, while constantly on the lookout for artistic talent in the direct environment. Others argue that to do something for the city necessitates an effort that needs to be paid for. According to this concept the neighborhood is relevant as an inspiration, an object to study, and as a spatial environment rather than a social network or target to be upgraded.

Moreover, social cohesion and creativity are not seen an obvious match. A neighborhood might also be aggressive and speak up against the presence of artists perceived as provocative and with lifestyles alien to the local culture. The housing associations recognize that the creative producers do not always fit in with the general culture of their residential blocks. 'It would not be acceptable for the janitor to suddenly find a sculpture of scrap material in the garden'.

Nevertheless, there need to be stepping stones for upcoming artists and artisans to practice stage performance and to test creations in front of small and friendly audiences in order to find out what works and what does not before taking the risk of presenting their art in front of a broader audience at high profile locations with corresponding entrance fees. (for comparison: a ticket for a concert at Poortgebouw costs €2,- while one for a concert at one of the main concert halls costs € 19 and more).

In the case of Rotterdam, the policy rather seems to be to have the creative economy exist on high profile urban islands. The high profile Creative City clusters in free-standing buildings like van Nelle or Creative Factory are not placed inside residential areas and do not aim to one day be embedded into a neighborhood.

"It's not only about buying the CD of „worldfamous" Pianist, but also hearing a Live- performance of a local artist. Nothing is better as live performances"
Saskia Sassen Hamburg 2009

Picture 3: 'Live in the livingroom' Rotterdam 2009

8. Creative Citizens Meet Urban Policies

The real estate market in Rotterdam has the lowest prices in the Netherlands and 8-10%

structural vacancy, a number that is more likely to increase than to go down. A real potential to transform unused space into a location of the creative city exists, though a number of barriers have to be overcome.

Market prices push the self-initiated creative clusters to the periphery of the town. A major disadvantage of such locations is the lack of public transport, especially at the weekends. This affects user groups who have strong community ties. Particularly (immigrant) groups that guard close control over the family reputation would not consider a potential creative career for their offspring, if it involves frequenting such locations. This is especially affecting young women with an immigration background who cannot afford a car and hesitate to participate in activities in the more difficult to access areas. For basically the same reason, spontaneous or small-scale events do not easily find a friendly public audience.

Accommodation in the creative sector often requires the concerned to overcome a whole host of problems, and a degree of informality. One central problem is that mixed use is often not allowed under mono zoning land-use plans. Places to meet soon turn into 'public places', for which strict Fire regulations apply. Those involved are usually unwilling to make the necessary investments in order to bring premises up to code without a long-term rental security and considering the often almost unaffordable rent levels.

For self-organizing clusters the planning system is hardly accessible. The 'Fabriek' became an example of the contradictory operations within the municipality, whose organization seems to be a landscape as diverse as the creative city itself. Local authorities (Deelgemeente) are the first possible public partners for creative initiatives, but they lack the means to act due to the complicated structure already mentioned. As part of the official Creative City policy, the urban real estate (OBR) and planning (dS+V) departments are geared towards facilitating the large, institutional clusters. Yet, in order to transform Rotterdam from a worker city to an intellectual metropolis, that is to

> *"increase the number of highly educated knowledge workers and creative entrepreneurs in town, and to create a tolerant, international urban cultural atmosphere"* (Creative City policy document)

all sorts of creativity are needed. The self-initiated creative clusters involve not only creative production but also constitute an important social capital, both for the creative producers as well as neighboring inhabitants. Even though frictions can rarely be avoided altogether sometimes new dialogues can be opened through low-threshhold projects run by local residents with surprisingly little effort. Creative City policies can be more effective, if they facilitate low-threshhold spaces to meet and to develop activities, to discover the world, to gain the feedback of others, and to experiment with the transfer of knowledge.

References

Economic Development Board Rotterdam (EDBR) & Development Agency (OBR) (2005) '*Rotterdam Economische Visie 2020*' [Vision for the Economy 2020] including The Executive Programme 2006-2009

Rotterdam Municipality (2007) '*Stadsvisie*' (Vision for the City 2030)

OntwikkelingsBedrijf Rotterdam (19 februari 2007) 'Visie Creatieve Economie 2007-2010' http://www.creativitystartshere.nl

COS, Centre for Statistics Rotterdam: http://www.cos.rotterdam.nl consulted October 2009, May 2010, November 2010

Florida in 't Gemaal: http://www.tentrotterdam.nl/shows/archief/20101111_florida_2.php Urban debate on Richard Florida and Rotterdam in 't Gemaal, 28 dec 2010

Marlet Gerard, Joost Poort Floks Laverman (2007) Atlas voor gemeenten (Atlas for Dutch Municipalities) edition 2007: culture VOC uitgevers www.atlasvoorgemeenten.nl/ *pdf consulted May 2010*

"Contrapolis; or, Creativity and Enclosure in the Cities" COnference Rotterdam 26th and 27th of March 2008 http://www.enoughroomforspace.org/projects/view/15?

Ministry Economic Affairs with Ministry of Education, Culture and Science: Creative value. Culture and economy paper 2009 Den Haag: MinEZ and MinOCW publication no. 09OI47

UNCTAD, Creative Economy Report 2008, UNCTAD, http://www.unctad.org/en/docs/ditc20082cer_en.pdf, (retrieved 28 dec 2010)

Websites of mentioned locations (in order of appearance):

http://www.ontwerpfabriek.nl/

http://www.schiecentrale.nl/

http://www.creativefactory.nl/

http://www.poortgebouw.nl/

http://www.wormweb.nl/

http://www.linckezwaerd.nl/

http://www.defabriek.nu/

http://creatiefbeheer.nl/

http://www.stichting-nac.nl/

6. From Growth to Quality: Less is Future

Sonja Beeck

In the first decade of the 21st century, some decisive indicators made it clear that we have to adjust our paradigms for urban development. Among others, Jeremy Rifkin recently announced the end of the oil era and forecast the third industrial revolution. It took the global financial crisis to get people to question growth as the one and only direction for development. In times of spatial polarization in Europe, a long term project at a small region in Eastern Germany shows remarkable results, namely the IBA Stadtumbau 2010. This project aims at demonstrating possible new and diverse methods for turning shrinkage into a creative process. Shrinkage occurs everywhere, in Japan as well as in the USA or in Finland, but during the past 20 years, Eastern Germany has witnessed the emergence of a particularly severe pattern of this phenomenon. The IBA Stadtumbau 2010 has provided a sort of testing ground, yielding lessons that can be useful for other regions that want to focus on improving quality of life without relying on constant growth.

After the German reunification, the eastern part of the country faced large-scale deindustrialization and the transformation from an industrial to a more service and knowledge based industry is still in progress. This is not particularly unusual in and by itself but in the case of Saxony-Anhalt the transformation brought and still brings with it an extreme decrease in population. Many residents, especially the young and well educated, already left to find new jobs in Western Germany or even abroad. New industries require a smaller workforce and new fields of employment are still developing. This process creates a state of insecurity for our cities. Shrinkage simultaneously infects all urban segments; the economy is down, social space is weakened by unemployment, poverty, and an aging population. The spatial impact is visible because shrinkage is not controlled and planners can not determine where it occurs. When such factors start to erode, new stimuli to trigger change are necessary. This is the moment when art as well as new communication strategies join in and the resulting interfacing between disciplines becomes a powerful source of change.

IBA Stadtumbau 2010

Within this framework of problems and questions a remarkable experiment started in 2003. The government of the state of Saxony-Anhalt started the International Building Exhibition urban redevelopment 2010. They enlisted the Bauhaus Dessau foundation and the state development company SALEG as partners for this IBA project, the first to be conducted for an entire state. It is a project which aims to develop diverse expertise to turn shrinkage into a creative process. Within a time frame of eight years, 19 cities worked hard to present their individual statement or solution for the problem. This year, in 2010, we will be presenting the results. It took quite some time, professional coaching, and experimental approaches in order to determine which creative possibilities exist that may guarantee the future of small and medium sized towns. In the beginning, the stigma of shrinkage weighed heavily on the mayors and other city leaders, who simply were not able to face their local community and openly discuss the problem. After a year of workshops, the attitudes began to shift and turned into energy focused on finding viable strategies. There were four core questions, which can probably be best understood with the aid of concrete examples:

1. What is the Most Important Local Trait or Resource to be Activated and Stabilized for the Future?

Koethen, a small town of 27,000 inhabitants, is famous for its free spirit and well-known thinkers have made Koethen their hometown. Johann Sebastian Bach composed the Brandenburg concerts there and Samuel Hahnemann, the father of homeopathy, lived and practiced in Koethen from 1821 to 1835. Homeopathy was discovered as on of Koethen's key images, a concept that could be a driving force in the economic and scientific development. Koethen, reclaimed by the worldwide community of homeopaths, has become the old and new capital of homeopathy and the European Library for Homeopathy was transferred from Hamburg to Koethen.

At the same time, Hahnemann's holistic approach to the intact and to the maladjusted organism gave rise to the question, if this method could not be transferred to urban planning and design. We founded an interdisciplinary workshop with city planners and a number of physicians and looked for a "patient". The Ludwigstrasse became the field of intervention. It was the first testing ground for the community to address a street with several vacant buildings holistically, to consider the impacts on the community and the space, and to develop thoughtful solutions and surprising methods to solve the problems. The "Coethener Methode" was found, a holistic strategy which transfers the homeopathic globuli into urban interventions which follow the principle of similarity. "Similis similibus currentur" means to work out a stimulus by provocation which activates energy for change in a complex system. All these experiences reached far beyond conventional urban marketing strategies. In Koethen, a city really "said goodbye" to an industrial future and turned to a future in healthcare, culture, and renewable energy and, through this process, tried to reactivate a hidden spirit.

The same happened in Lutherstadt Wittenberg, a Unesco World Heritage Site, the former sphere of activity of the reformer Martin Luther, and, nowadays, a rich educational landscape with numerous scientific, cultural, and confessional institutions of learning. Through the IBA they succeeded in forming a non-university campus. They connected the local institutions on a strong platform of shared interest and the resulting synergy has triggered spatial development. It was possible to refurbish many historic buildings, which now can be used again to host guests, or conferences, or creative classes. Koethen as well as Lutherstadt Wittenberg each found a perfect way to reactivate the cities' respective heritages to look forward to a bright future.

2. How Can a Smart Solution for the Spatial Results of Shrinkage be Found?

Dessau is the IBA city with the most radical approach. During its industrial era the city grew enormously. Today, it faces a population decline of around 30%. Due to major destruction during World War II there is a lack of a stable center that could act as an "anchor" around which the city could reduce its size. Therefore, Dessau decided to shrink into an archipelago of dense and stable islands with green zones in between. This makes a lot of sense insofar as Dessau is surrounded by the Dessau-Woerlitz Garden Realm (Dessau's second Unesco World Heritage Site besides the Bauhaus) and people identify themselves with the landscape as part of their town.

We started with a master plan for demolition. Fierce negotiations took place but in the end this process failed due to the conflicting aims of the real estate industry and the housing stock. We developed a more process oriented strategy and over time, as buildings are torn down, the landscape zones will gradually emerge. It is essential for the success that citizens are involved into this process to constantly discuss questions of aesthetics, area management, care and the new value of urban life which comes along with the new landscape zones.

Aschersleben decided to shrink in the classic way from the outside to the inside. They carefully protected the historic center and demolished the *Plattenbauten* at the edges. The most problematic zone was the belt highway surrounding the historic center. Through the IBA we slowly transformed this "tunnel of horror" into highly creative space. Supermarkets and pit stops went in to provide adequate infrastructure for urban life in the 21st century, its most prominent feature, an old factory, was transformed into a school with a special focus on creativity, and, in 2004, Germany's first "Drive Thru Gallery" was founded. Over time, various art installations filled the vacant spaces between buildings, which can be viewed from vehicles on this busy street that defines the edge of the city center.

3. How Can as Many Citizens as Possible be Involved in the Projects and the Responsibility Shared among Them?

In Lutherstadt Eisleben, the town where Martin Luther was born and died, the IBA slogan "cleverer, cooperative, more compact," has been created. This slogan mirrors the spirit of the IBA movement. Together with all involved, and sometimes conflicting parties they lead discussions that can result in decisions with fabulous results. The Luther Trail as well as a number of new museums are flagships in the IBA Stadtumbau 2010. Quite possibly the most sustainable result though can be seen in the way all partners in Lutherstadt Eisleben learned to work together and set up a fruitful and cooperative planning process. It may very well be that the process leading to a desired result becomes all the more important in times of limited resources .

4. How Should the Most Significant Questions for the Future be Addressed?

Some of the nineteen IBA cities also raised fundamental questions regarding the foundations of urban society, which, generally speaking, also start to erode in times of demographic change and shrinkage. Bernburg realized that a good education in combination with substantial training for the job is essential for the economic structure of and stability within a local community. Some companies had already complained about a new generation of employees with a noticeably lower level of education. Also, the statistics show an alarming rate of high school dropouts. These facts led Bernburg to the idea to work out a concept for a new school in the heart of the city. Schools located further to the edge of the city will be closed over a period of time and instead the new Campus Technicus will be set up in close cooperation with the local theater, library, church, music school, as well as other institutions. Bernburg aims at strengthening education and culture as a solid foundation for urban society.

The smallest city in the IBA, Wanzleben (5000 inhabitants), set its focus on the notion of *family*. Facing a low birthrate as well as a progressively fragmented and individualized society, the traditional idea of what exactly constitutes a *family* has to be questioned. They worked on projects aimed at stabilizing the social networks within the small city in order to be able to provide fallback solutions whenever more conventional social structures collapse. The "city as a family" is admittedly utopian; it is, nonetheless, a perfectly reasonable question to ask which organizational functions of families can or could be transferred to a wider group in a small town.

Summary

The small cities in Saxony-Anhalt mentioned above are good examples for the hypothesis that the purely growth-oriented criteria for success have to be redefined. The IBA cities learned to develop new options to find opportunities for the future.

The first lesson everybody had to learn was to open up and to discuss the difficult situation in public and to get rid of the commonly stigmatized notion of shrinkage. The problems were not their fault; there was no reason for depression or resignation but for smart action, creative strategies, and common decisions.

Local residents had to think deeply about their town's strategic vision and potential. They experienced that complex problems could only be solved in a more integrated culture of communication. Workshops, round tables, and cross-disciplinary work groups are all necessary to find smart solutions. The highest potential for creativity was found when different disciplines interfaced. To shrink means to negotiate goals and budgets in a very serious way and it is extremely helpful to involve all affected parties in the negotiation process right from the start. The integrating effect of a project creates positive side-effects for those who are engaged in it, such as for example a positive atmosphere and work spirit. The size of a project, whether a building or an event is concerned, is not all that important. The sense of "doing something together" is important for community building, which is not a romantic idea but pure necessity in a shrinking town. Participation means to take on responsibility and activate all kinds of forces within the community. Those cities that developed a master vision for themselves (German: Leitbild) where successful.

In the last eight years, planning theory gave repeatedly rise to the notion that the era of master plans is over and that the secret for city planners is to design custom made processes. It is not difficult to design a process though; the most important and most difficult aspect is to work through the process as a whole. In every city there are peaks and valleys, happiness and horrible fights. It required a lot of sensitivity and diplomacy as well as a long breath to guide the projects and processes through the storm. Smart cities write down their most important goals and priorities to give them a chance to survive even the next election period; smart cities can also say no to investors and others who want to realize projects that are not in line with the community vision.

Today, development must be triggered from the bottom up and sheltered from the top down. It requires a high level of personal engagement and an empathic attitude from everybody involved. If the process is successful, new confidence will be the most important success and confidence comes out of the experience that they (the cities) worked hard to multiply their options and that there is a future beyond industrial growth.

7. Mobility in the In-between City: Getting Stuck between the Local and the Global [1]

Roger Keil

1. Introduction: The Metropolitan Century

In a world that is predominantly urban, attention of urban research and practice now moves inevitably to the forms and social formations that exist in the expanding metropolitan regions of the globe. Where and how do people in cities really live? The acceleration of the urban transition has opened up the question what kinds of built forms and social relationships will emerge in a society which does not just statistically count most people in cities but also sees an even larger majority engaged in urban ways of life. If we agree that urbanization is the defining social process of the emerging century, we might ask what consequences that process has on the ground where people live.

Clearly, urbanization means different things to different urbanites. Worldwide most people who are currently becoming urban are actually becoming suburban, whether it is life in high rise settlements, single family home subdivisions, gated communities, or squatter settlements. But suburbanization and suburbanism are changing shape. New forms of in-betweenness are prevalent. In this paper, I will look at the case of Canada, and more specifically at the country's largest city, Toronto. Close to 80 percent of Canadians reside in cities. What is more, most Canadians live in large urban areas in the south of the country, predominantly along the US-Canadian border. Over the past few decades, Canadian towns that had grown on the country's wealth of resources have, with the exception of a few oil based settlements like Ft. McMurray in the West, dwindled in population size and significance while large urban centers, in particular Toronto, Montreal, and Vancouver, have grown as post-industrial service centers and global cities which attract most international investment, cultural flows, and immigration. A new type of urbanization has surely emerged with some arguing that Canada has now become an "urban nation" (Broadbent 2008). Where cities used to be alien outposts in an agricultural and resource based society, they are now considered the engines of a globally oriented, "creative" economy. Typically, urban policy in Canada's largest city, Toronto, for example, is propelled by images of reurbanization, cultural renaissance, tourism, and bohemian lifestyles. Most of the focus of the elites that shape the cities is on the glittering downtown areas, where museums, condominiums, art galleries, entertainment and sports complexes, and waterfront revitalization takes place (Lehrer, Keil, Kipfer 2010).

Still, as I will argue in this short essay, the focus on the inner city may hide a more important feature of the metropolitan society as which Canada now recognizes itself. While the inner city retains large percentages of the region's population and jobs, and while the classical outer residential suburbs continue to attract often young, often immigrant families in a regional real estate market that pushes the demand for large and affordable housing to the cookie-cutter subdivisions beyond an hour's distance from the core of the urban region (Fiedler and Addie 2008), there is another urban settlement form that gets less attention than it should. The urban century is in-between. For most Canadians, across the country but most visibly perhaps in the

DISCUSSION PAPER

vast urban expanse of the Greater Golden Horseshoe of the Toronto region, living in the city means living in a newly emerging form of suburbanization which defies the classical patterns of both post-war peripheral settlements and downtown life. Most Canadians now live, work, and play in what German planner Tom Sieverts has called the *Zwischenstadt*, an in-between city (2003). Between the traditional downtown and the conventional suburb, the topology of the in-between city takes shape.

Sieverts' notion of *Zwischenstadt* was originally based on recent spatial developments in Europe. It entailed a critique of concepts of the traditional, more compact, uni-centred European city. Sieverts notes that this new urban form is now pervasive and home as well as workplace to a growing percentage of Europeans. The in-between cities now appear as the most dynamic and problematic forms of suburbanization. Following Sieverts' original idea, the concept of the in-between city denotes a new urban and regional form 'which is neither city nor landscape' (Sieverts 2003, 3). Different from both the old central city and the traditional suburb, the in-between city is 'diffuse' and 'gives an "unplanned" impression' (Sieverts 2003, 3). And Sieverts continues: 'All this taken together produces a carpet of settlement which appears to be without any plan but has the nature of a palimpsest in which old, superfluous and deleted text and images glimmer through the new text' (Sieverts 2003, 5-6)

For our analysis, we have adapted Sieverts' concept to Canada, where the in-between comprises the old post-WWII suburbs in particular but also the transitional zones between those suburbs and the exurban fringe. As we have explained in greater detail elsewhere (Young, Wood and Keil 2011a; Young and Keil 2009), they typically encompass utility corridors, conservation areas, large urban landscape forms such as oil tank farms, military sites, municipal airports, industrial facilities, large scale housing estates, often public, marginal agricultural lands, as well as ravines, woodlots, and retention ponds, new strip malls, university or other educational institutions, infrastructures such as rail switching yards or freight terminals, landfills (sometimes expired), entertainment facilities such as theme parks and movieplexes, and also big box retail outlets, religiously oriented developments, etc. They also contain small pockets of hugely diversified urban uses such as ethnic mini-malls, mini-ghettos of students or poverty populations, rich enclaves, semi-legal uses such as strip clubs and saunas, as well as niche market entertainment locales such as climbing walls or go-cart tracks. They include a wild and often unexplainable mix of uses untypical for either the inner city or the classical suburb; they present landscapes of extreme spatial and social segregation. For a research project, sponsored by Infrastructure Canada and the Toronto Community Housing Company, just concluded at the City Institute at York University we selected an area of 85km^2 that we thought most typically represented the in-between mix. That area lies partly in the City of Toronto and partly in the City of Vaughan, is home to about 150,000 people, and is a place that is rich in social and physical complexities and contradictions.

Conceptually, using the in-between lens presents a particular view towards urban Canada. It carves out a piece from the urban landscape that usually remains invisible between the glam-

[1] Research for this paper has been funded by a grant under the direction of Roger Keil, Patricia Wood, and Douglas Young. The project is called "In-between Infrastructure: Urban Connectivity in an Age of Vulnerability". It was sponsored under the Peer Reviewed Research Studies (PRRS) program of Infrastructure Canada. Some financial support was also provided by Toronto Community Housing Company, one of the community partners to the project.

or zones that govern urban policy and research. It highlights what Graham and Marvin have called "splintering urbanism" (Graham and Marvin, 2001), a term which is especially relevant when viewing the urban region from the point of view of infrastructure as we will do below. The idea of a splintering urban fabric corresponds to other recent spatial concepts that have bearing on our thinking here. Hajer and Reijndorp, for example have described urban regions as "archipelagos of enclaves" (Hajer and Reijndorp, 2001).

The in-between city is a combination of obsolescence and overburdening through the state as infrastructures of housing and transportation have been laid out in planned and sometimes authoritarian ways. This has occurred over the past sixty years as a mix of at first Fordist-Keynesian and later post-Fordist state interventions. But the in-between city is also a place of rampant market activity as developers and place entrepreneurs have pursued their profit interests through the production of the in-between landscape. The creation of marginality in a period of advanced neoliberalization proceeds along a register of welfare state retreat/destruction, market oriented policy, etc. which is somewhat universal in advanced capitalist countries but also specific to place (Young, Wood and Keil, 2011b; Boudreau, Keil, and Young, 2009).

In our view, the in-between city is less a spatial form that can be defined in static positive terms (fixed average densities, specific constitutive elements, particular minimal features, mix of uses, etc.) but a set of internal and external relationships that realign the elements of urbanity more fundamentally. When we propose to consider in-betweenness as relationality, we see it as part of

- the rescaling of socio-spatial relationships in the globalizing city region
- a reordering of socio-demographic and socio-economic relationships
- a recalibration of the relationships of labour and life, of workplace and housing
- the reorganization of urban political ecology of the city region (Keil and Young 2010).

The in-between study area displays idiosyncratic decentralization such as state-led and developer driven forms of suburbanization that mesh with the initiative of residents to produce quirky ensembles of everyday livability. But there is also emerging centrality. York University with its 50,000 students and many thousand employees is such a place of emergent centrality, buttressed by subway expansion plans that will connect the suburban campus to the exurbs where many students live but also to the downtown. Such centrality also manifests itself in the curious development of Canada's only urban national park, in the south of our study area. A former military base and waning production site of the aerospace industry, Downsview Park has now become a focal point for a central park-type experiment which could shift the way in which we view the production of space in the Toronto region in the future.

The study area is characterized by dramatic structural inequalities in infrastructure provision and service delivery. In this pre-subway period, the most massive investments have been in roads. The area is bounded by three major highways that connect the Toronto region's more valued spots, from which drivers use the in-between city as a mere by-pass and thoroughfare.

East-West connection as part of the overall trans-section of Canada, the link to the international airport and the exurban post-Fordist economy, as well as the North-South commuter links that serve the urban economy have to date taken precedence over the home-grown needs of the in-between city.

While being radically underserved and unequally provisioned with infrastructures, many residents of the in-between city are vulnerable to unpredictable events, be they environmental, economic, or social. They tend to be poorer and less auto-mobile than the rest of the urban population. They are more likely to be non-white and immigrant, and they are, to a high degree, tenants. As far as the in-between city overlaps with the old inner suburbs of Toronto, its residents share the problems identified by University of Toronto researchers for the third of Toronto's population that is growing poorer and more segregated (Hulchanski 2006). The vulnerabilities and risks for urban populations in Toronto's in-between city are co-generated by the failure of conventional political spaces and processes to capture the connectivities threaded through those places that are in-between the center and exurbia. The in-between city combines the problems of the classical suburb with the problems of not-yet-developed areas and magnetically attracts the "urban" problems of congestion, poverty, racism, etc.

2. Infrastructure and the In-between City

For the remainder of this paper, I will turn my attention to the infrastructure of the in-between city. I am guided here by the assumption that understanding the infrastructure problems of the "in-between city" is a necessary precondition for creating more sustainable and socially just urban regions, and for designing a system of social and cultural infrastructure that has everything a community needs and which meets global needs as well.

Infrastructure builds cities as it allows connections between the major functions of the urban region to be filled in where roads, sewers, communication and energy networks, mostly large technological systems (Monstadt 2009), have created the skeleton of development. But largely as a function of how these infrastructures are built, they also dissolve cities as they create centrifugal possibilities. A global "suburban solution" (Walker, 1981) drains the urban centers and leads to new forms of concentration where there are no traditional accumulations of infrastructure services. In recent decades, infrastructure investment facilitated largely a more pervasively sprawled metropolitan landscape entirely dedicated to providing the most efficient conduit for global capital. Even in overall "healthy" metropolitan regions (such as Toronto) the centrifugal dynamics continue. In Toronto, for example, the recent census figures suggest an unbroken, if not accelerated trend towards suburbanization of housing and jobs. This has social and spatial implications: The traditional focus on collective consumption is partially replaced with a purely exchange value oriented set of criteria for infrastructure development which makes global economic competitiveness, rather than local social cohesion, the marker of success (Young and Keil 2009).

Infrastructure is built, financed, and provided for the connection of prime network spaces (Graham and Marvin, 2001). Apart from serving those needs, little attention has traditionally been paid to the spaces that are traversed in the process of connecting the splintered premium locales of the metropolitan region. Politically, this is supported by conspiring exurban voters and downtown interests alike. It is in their shared interest to create better bypasses of the in-between city in order to move goods and people more efficiently from one premium space to another. The infrastructure of the in-between city is there to be transgressed at high speed to reach other points in the urban region.

Infrastructure in the evolving socio-spatial landscape of the "in-between city" consequently provides a curious mix of mobility and immobility, accessibility and connectivity, particularly in and through transportation. Much of the in-between urban landscape is a product of planning but there are also accidental developments. The peculiar mixture that characterizes this dynamic part of today's metropolitan region poses a specific set of challenges. These areas are often meant to perform locally and globally scaled functions side by side without infrastructural arrangements in place to support these services. From this tension spring particular conflicts, vulnerabilities, and contradictions that need to be taken up by city planning and politics in order to provide the necessary socio-spatial cohesion.

The possibility of a radically altered way of conceiving the region from the perspective of infrastructure connectivity in which the in-between cities are *not* bypassed leads to urgent questions. Will the global economic recession reinforce the ways in which the in-between infrastructures and their dependent populations have been marginalized or will they participate in the renewal? How will infrastructure be used in the rebuilding of urban economies? Will the in-between city develop a political voice alongside the traditional power centers downtown and in the suburbs?

As we have discussed at greater length elsewhere (Young, Wood, and Keil 2011b), the politics of the in-between entails a shift in metropolitan politics from the central and suburban poles where they are usually located and institutionalized. This would mean concentrating on the in-between spaces that are overlooked in real policy regimes, territorial politics, and conceptual frameworks. Such a shift may open up new perspectives on the city region and its politics overall. The centrality of the state and the market in structuring the arena of urban politics has to be supplemented by what Sieverts (2003, 69) has called "the organisation of everyday living space." We can thus move the focus of urban politics away from the traditional center-suburb dichotomy and create a new perspective. Rather than viewing peripheries and centers as distinct or the former as a derivative of the latter we now point to their relationships at the core of urban political space. Urban politics of the in-between city happens predominantly in the conventional modes of the municipal arena. Councilors, planners, and public officials play a game everyone knows the rules to. The boundaries between public and private are respected and property values are safeguarded. Such politics runs on 'non-decision making' and is geared towards a functioning marketplace of service provision, planning, and city building. The normal politics of local affairs is also scaled to fit the technical parameters of public services: water, waste, transportation, etc. This would need to be different in the politics we advocate in the in-between city. Instead, citizens are being heard; they organize themselves, speak to their neighbors, and protest. The politics of the in-between city, then, breaks the mold of local politics and challenges the framework in which 'issues' are usually packaged. It also runs up against common parochialisms in urban politics and the classed and racialized containers of such politics. The horizon of politics under these circumstances is narrow and tied to very special interests (home ownership, class privilege, etc.). A new politics of mobility and infrastructure in the in-between city must make boundaries an issue. Such politics would be a reflection of a complex urbanized life which poses new challenges for politics and planning in the entire city. The mixed places that produce such new socio-spatial relations and their mobility needs are here to stay. Most of them will establish themselves in some kind of middle kingdom of immigration, de- and reindustrialization and 'anaesthetic landscape' (Sieverts, 2007a). It is from the crisis-prone and disaster-triggered in-between city that we might have to re-imagine politics of the possible that governs the metropolis. Sieverts notes that current planning doctrine tends to "exclude different, complementary, more complex modes of thinking" and doubts whether they should "still be made the guideline of urbanist and political praxis" (Sieverts, 2011: 11) and that the in-between city is still "unloved particularly by planners and opinion makers and it is disregarded by urban design, planning and politics" (Sieverts, 2011: 20). He proposes to move the spatial imaginary of a "fragmented urban landscape" into the center of the political challenge of metropolitan governance and voices his "intention to approach the in-between city as the life space of the majority of the population with critical sympathy and responsibility and to detect the opportunities of a qualification of this still young urban forms, which will be under great pressure of transformation in the next historical phase based on the demographic development of globalization and the preparation for a period of post-fossilist forms of energy" (Sieverts, 2011: 20). Despite the current centrality of the in-between forms of urbanity, little is done to confront the growing planning and governance challenges through "comprehensiveresponsibility" (Sieverts, 2011: 23).

Sieverts favors the "interpretation of the urban region as a field in steady transition… for it leads directly to the 'material' forces, as the 'raw material' of design". And he continues, "In this interpretation as an urban fabric in steady transition, one can emphasise the continuation of the old urban traditions, or you can, in contrast, look at the '*Zwischenstadt*' as a field of new developments, as a new frontier of experiments and innovations. Both interpretations are legitimized, as the '*Zwischenstadt*' is a field of '*Gleichzeitigkeit des Ungleichzeitigen*' (the simultaneity of different eras)" (Sieverts, 2007a: 207). The transitional character of the *Zwischenstadt* is not just one of urban development periods but also needs to be read in the context of the "epochal and global ecological crisis" during which these "young urban landscapes will have to change profoundly" (Sieverts, 2007b, 9). Sieverts explains that the generational turnover of existing infrastructure is imminent and leads to positive possibilities as "in the coming years their built structures enter their first 'natural' renovation cycle, which can be used for a far-reaching reconstruction. The big infrastructure must also be renewed and must partly be retooled for ecological reasons by switching it to new systems such as, for example, certain systems of sewage treatment, energy and transportation" (Sieverts, 2007b, 9). This kind of hope is pinned, in Toronto, on the massive proposal of former Mayor Miller's Tower Renewal campaign, the goal of which is the renovation of about 1,000 high rise rental apartment buildings which were built throughout Toronto's suburbs in the 1960s and 70s. It is equally important to keep alive the spirit of the Transit City plan which, although politically on shaky ground, purports to change the very logic of the city's public transportation network from a center-heavy system that privileges prime network spaces to a more democratic form of mobility that would, among other things, connect the more socially marginalized areas of the in-between city.

3. Conclusions: "Politics of Infrastructure"

Answering the call for a new politics of infrastructure that takes the in-between city seriously presupposes at a minimum to acknowledge these communities' existence beyond neo-colonial gestures from the political high ground of the central city. A new "politics of infrastructure" must start from the growing awareness that "governing and experiencing the fabric of the city" (McFarlane and Rutherford 2008: 363) involves political acts that produce and reproduce the infrastructures of urban regions. A subsequent "politicization of infrastructure" (ibid.) rests on the understanding of how infrastructure policies and planning are linked to "the co-evolution of cities and technical networks in a global context" (McFarlane and Rutherford 2008: 365). The politicization of infrastructures therefore includes the politicization of the people in the in-between city around issues of transportation, infrastructure, and connectivity on the basis of their own experienced needs of mobility and access. If a new politics in this sense can be inserted into the mobility discourse of the in-between city, the communities in this emerging (sub)urban landscape may be able to get out of their status of being literally stuck between the local and the global.

References

Boudreau, Julie-Anne, Roger Keil, and Douglas Young. 2009 *Changing Toronto: Governing Urban Neoliberalism*. Toronto: University Toronto Press.

Broadbent, Alan. 2008. *Urban Nation: Why We Need to Give Power Back to the Cities to Make Canada Strong*. Toronto: Harper Collins Publishers Ltd.

Fiedler, R. and Jean-Paul Addie. 2008 'Canadian Cities on the Edge: Reassessing the Canadian Suburb' *City Institute at York University Occasional Paper Series*, 1 (available at http://www.yorku.ca/city/Publications/OccasionalPapers/index.html)

Graham, S. and Marvin, S. 2001. *Splintering Urbanism: Networked Infrastructures, Technological Mobilities and the Urban Condition*. London: Routledge.

Hajer, Maarten, and Arnold Reijndorp. 2001. *In Search of New Public Domain*. Rotterdam: NAi Publisher.

Hulchanski, David. 2006 The Suburbanization of the non-gentry: the Impoverishment and Racialization of Toronto's Inner Suburbs. Toronto: Centre for Urban and Community Studies.

Keil, Roger, and Douglas Young. 2010. Introduction: In-Between Canada -- The Emergence of the New Urban Middle, In Young, Douglas, Patricia Wood and Roger Keil eds. 2010. *In-Between Infrastructure: Urban Connectivity in an Age of Vulnerability*. Kelowna, BC: Praxis(e) Press.

Lehrer, Ute, Roger Keil, and Stefan Kipfer. 2010. Reurbanization in Toronto: Condominium boom and social housing revitalization, *disP. The Planning Review*, Vol 46, 1, Issue 180, 81-90.

McFarlane, Colin and Jonathan Rutherford. 2008. Political Infrastructures: Governing and Experiencing the Fabric of the City, *International Journal of Urban and Regional Research* 32,2; 363-74.

Monstadt, Jochen. 2009. Conceptualizing the Political Ecology of Urban Infrastructures: Insights from Technology and Urban Studies. *Environment and Planning A*.

Sieverts, Thomas 2003. *Cities Without Cities: An Interpretation of the Zwischenstadt*. London: Spon Press.

Sieverts, Thomas 2007a. Some notes on aesthetics in a "städtebau" on a regional scale. In, R. Heil, A. Kaminski, M. Stippak, A. Unger & M. Ziegler (eds.), *Tensions and Convergences - Technological and Aesthetic Transformations of Society*. Bielefeld/Piscataway: Transcript & Transaction, pp. 199-212.

Sieverts, Thomas. 2007b. Von der unmöglichen Ordnung zu einer möglichen Unordnung im Entwerfen der Stadtlandschaft, *DISP* 169: 5-16.

Sieverts, Thomas 2011. Planning In-Between, In: Young, Douglas, Patricia Wood and Roger Keil eds. 2011. *In-Between Infrastructure: Urban Connectivity in an Age of Vulnerability*. Kelowna, BC: Praxis(e) Press.

Walker, R. 1981. A Theory of Suburbanization: Capitalism and the Construction of Urban Space in the United States. In Urbanization and Urban Planning under Advanced Capitalist Societies, ed. M. Dear and A. Scott, New York: Methuen.

Young, D. & Keil, R. 2009. Reconnecting the Disconnected: The Politics of Infrastructure in the In-between City, *Cities*, 27, 2, April, Pages 87-95

Young, Douglas, Patricia Wood, and Roger Keil eds. 2011a. *In-Between Infrastructure: Urban Connectivity in an Age of Vulnerability*. Kelowna, BC: Praxis(e) Press.

Young, Douglas, Patricia Wood, and Roger Keil eds. 2011b. Conclusion: From critique to politics and planning. In: Young, Douglas, Patricia Wood and Roger Keil eds. *In-Between Infrastructure: Urban Connectivity in an Age of Vulnerability*. Kelowna, BC: Praxis(e) Press.

8. Neoliberal Hypermobility and the Tricycle

Glen Norcliffe

Although a degree of mobility is essential for human survival, some residents of the modern city have become excessively mobile. Of course, people need to move around the city as part of everyday life, but in the neoliberal age a minority are making mobility a fetish by engaging in excessive movement. John Adams (1999) has adopted the metaphor of *hypermobility* to describe this pattern of extreme travel: he argues that while mobility can be liberating and empowering, rapid growth in the numbers of people over-exercising that freedom is damaging the planet and exacerbating the risks of contemporary global capitalism (Beck, 1992). This trend might simply be attributed to technological improvements which have accelerated mobility over the decades, in some cases to such an extent that the Sustainability of the city in its present form is put into question (Lemon, 1996). I suggest, however, that technology alone does not explain this tendency towards hypermobility; in the neoliberal age citizens engaged in the pursuit of modernity are using hypermobility as one of the ways of establishing their credentials as modern world citizens. By travelling frequently to diverse events, these travellers are signalling their positionality as members of the global elite.

The development of new modes of transport during the industrial age led the modern city to grow in particular ways. Tramways, streetcars, electric railways, the automobile and air transportation allowed cities to grow in various ways. My focus – cycling – is a mode of transport that often falls below the radar in studies of mobility, although there is increasing awareness of the potential of *cycling* as a clean, silent, swift and low cost means of movement(Furness, 2010).

1. Argument

In his classic book, *Civilisation and its Discontents*, Sigmund Freud (1929) argued that humans are instinctively possessive, and aggressive towards competitors. These traits run counter to civilisation's need for individuals to conform to certain social norms and to repress these selfish instincts by sharing, acting peacefully, and respecting the wishes of others. Civilisation punishes individuals who do not obey community laws, and rewards those who do. Freud sees discontent arising from the pressure on individuals to conform to the law by suppressing their more selfish instincts. Freud's notion of discontent was taken up by Joseph Stiglitz in his more recent book on *Globalization and its Discontents* (2002) in which he turns round Freud's argument by proposing that, in the neoliberal age, it is civilisation that has reason to be discontented, especially since the policies of the IMF, WTO, the World Bank, and of many governments favour possessiveness, aggression towards competitors, and self-reward, all traits that, in Freud's view, run counter to the priorities of civilisation.

I wish to take up one very particular aspect of the tension between individual traits and community social values as they relate to mobility in the city. In general, this tension is self-evident: can drivers go wherever they wish, as fast as they wish, with whomever they wish? Or, do drivers have to conform to various social norms? The particular version of this tension to be explored in this essay is the contrast between one account of the bicycle which sees it as an instrument of modernity that contributes in a small way to hypermobility, and another version of the bicycle as a functional and social vehicle whose use conforms to broader societal goals. During the past century the bicycle has promoted *modernity* as a racing machine (on and off roads), as an expensive and highly visible class marker, as the most efficient conveyance for commuters and shoppers, as a superior means of delivering goods, and for the flâneur on wheels as a way of being seen as a modern citizen. Paradoxically, at other times and in other places the bicycle has played a role in resisting modern tendencies as an environmentally-friendly conveyance, as a means of escaping to quiet spaces, as a tool for conviviality when riding in social groups, and as a low-cost but slower way of delivering goods.

The late Victorian era of imperialism and liberal free-trade was one of very marked inequalities of wealth and incomes, comparable to those that have been re-createdsian-welfare age when the combined trauma of the Great Depression and the Second World War created a consensus in favour of more egalitarian policies. For Victorians, cycle ownership was a class marker separating the wealthy from the poor. Cycling was restricted to those with the means to make the initial acquisition, and then to purchase all the accessories as well as joining a cycling club (Norcliffe, 2006). Bicycle and tricycle technology evolved rapidly throughout the Victorian era moving from wooden wheeled velocipedes to the high wheel bicycle and then the pneumatic safety bicycle. The manufacture of cycles was located exclusively in western countries; it was mainly concentrated geographically in local and regional clusters where new technologies were developed (Norcliffe, 2009), and where specialist sub-contractors gathered close to the main cycle assemblers. The discontents at this stage formed a small minority who were essentially anti-moderns fearful either that bicycles would threaten their livelihood, or compete in spaces which they had previously monopolized.

Today, the versatility of the cycle results in quite different cycling practices in different settings, giving rise to complex histories and geographies so that the bicycle has a big range of meanings in different contexts, some of which favour the pursuit of individual traits, while others advance the interests of collectivities. For a minority seeking greater speed or more thrills, a sub-set of high-end bicycles continues the pursuit of modernity by incorporating the newest technologies. But for a growing number of users it is welcomed as an earth friendly technology that reduces some of the dangers of contemporary risk capitalism (Beck, 2009). But this summation needs qualifying, for it depends on the circumstances.

2. Tricycles and Mobility in the Late Nineteenth Century

In 1877 a British inventor, James Starley, developed and/or patented three quite different tricycles which in turn launched a little recognized tricycle boom dating from 1877 to 1886. Each of these tricycles was adapted to carry freight or passengers such that the carrier tricycle soon became a significant novelty on the streets of western cities. By performing the newest technology very visibly on city streets, these tricycles drew favourable attention to the firms whose names were neatly written on them. A horse drawing a delivery van carried a far greater load, and when whipped up could travel as fast as the carrier tricycle. But a horse was commonplace, whereas a carrier tricycle was not, and it did not need watering or feeding or a stable, nor did it mess up the streets. The tricycle was viewed as a clean modern technology.

From the late 1870s on, the carrier tricycle was used extensively in western cities. Not surprisingly it lost much of its novelty value by the end of the nineteenth century, but it was still widely used as a functional vehicle in the first half of the twentieth century. Its advantages were its flexibility, low operating costs, ability to move fairly quickly along most roads and cycleways, and the ease with which its rider could interact with the public *en route* and promote his or his employer's interests. Only in the 1950s, with the increasing use of motor vehicles, did the working tricycle disappear in Western Europe, with the ice-cream tricycle the last to go.

3. Tricycles and Mobility in the Twenty-first Century

Although the working tricycle largely disappeared from the landscape of western countries soon after the Second World War, it was entering its prime in many Asian and African countries as a means of urban transportation for people (the pedicab) and as a vehicle for delivering a wide range of goods. My remarks are based on observing working tricycles in several Chinese cities between 2007 and 2009. Chinese roadways generally have four rights of way, two central ways for motorised vehicles which move quite fast but are frequently jammed. On each side there is a roadway dedicated to bicycles, carts, carrier tricycles and everything else – typically moving at around 15 kph - which is rarely blocked by jams. This arrangement has become institutionalized and is usually the model for new streets, but not for major arterial roads such as the ring roads of major cities from which slow-moving vehicles are excluded. Motor traffic moves rapidly on arterial roads, but traffic jams are frequent, especially during the rush hours: average vehicle speeds in city centres are probably about the same as those of bicycles.

Carrier tricycles are widely used in China. Almost every farm has one. In cities they are used to transport a huge variety of goods and as mobile shops. Nearly all road and public garden maintenance is done by using these carrier tricycles. Perhaps most important of all is the amount of urban rubbish gathered with these tricycles, almost all of it recycled, creating one of the most effective low-cost recycling systems in the world. And, as already noted, these tricycles also serve as various forms of pedicabs. They are very effective in short haul journeys, particularly along congested and narrow streets. Data on the number of working tricycles in China do not appear to be published, but a crude estimate of between 40 and 60 million working tricycles in China seems reasonable, which roughly matches the number of private cars.

A high percentage of China's citizens are engaged wholeheartedly in efforts to modernize the country and catch up on time lost during the Cultural Revolution. Under China's developmental state, neoliberal practices are accepted with enthusiasm, although carefully managed by the People's Republic. Arguably, no other economy has embraced globalization so extensively, such that China is now the world's largest exporter of manufactured goods as well as the largest buyer of Western debt. The luxury cars and modern houses of the rapidly emerging business class are highly visible. The negative consequences of the rapid growth of infrastructure, utilities and manufacturing industries have been generally accepted in China as unfortunate but necessary part of the catch-up.

My interest in the carrier tricycles of China led local citizens to express puzzlement at why I was recording vestiges of the old China instead of focussing on the new and hypermobile China. Advantages of the humble carrier tricycle include adding almost no pollution, moving swiftly on congested city streets, accessing narrow lanes and alleyways, providing employment for many rural migrants with very limited skills, and as a low-cost machine for collecting recycled materials. My suggestion that an up-dated version might be part of China's future was usually met with scepticism or disbelief.

4. Discontentment

The *green city* is a project that has entered planning discourses and planning practices only during the past 25 years. This recent shift in city planning is attributable to growing awareness of the likely trajectory and consequences of uncontained city modernization. Paradoxically, the rise of postmodern sentiments, the culture of preservation, and concerns for the quality of life and liveability of the city accelerated at the same time that Keynesian welfare politics were being supplanted by neoliberal nostrums.

The carrier tricycle has obvious advantages in a green city, especially in a low-income country. Yet there is little audible discontent with the on-going project to modernize these countries; rather there is enormous enthusiasm to engage in modern life, and get rid of the older vestiges. In 1998, for instance, the city of Wuhan banned the use of carrier tricycles on the grounds that they were dangerous and polluting (some have tiny 2 stroke engines). Being modern is a legitimate aspiration, but if we are to build green cities, then in the case of mobility there is a need for a more pluralistic approach since cyclists have a competitive advantage at the neighbourhood scale. Technological innovation is going on in this field –for example in 2009 in Tianjin I rode a new form of short wheelbase tricycle with a geared front wheel drive designed for seniors. For the present, discontent with neoliberal mobility seems to come mainly from within OECD states where the negative externalities of hypermobility are most in evidence.

5. Conclusion

Whereas Freud was concerned with the discontent of individuals who bucked the rules of civilization, Stiglitz is concerned that free-market global practices of the neoliberal era may weaken civilization itself and promote financial crises. One corollary of neoliberal globalization is the hypermobility of a small group of individuals, which increases the risk of: polarisation between rich and poor; less convivial communities; less cultural variation; increased risk to pedestrians; and reduced health and fitness (Adams, 2010).

This theme was explored in the context of the carrier tricycle. This three-wheeled vehicle was in the vanguard of modernity in the late Victorian era. It then became a utility vehicle which was to prove its worth for the next 50 years in western countries, before being eclipsed by motor vehicles. Meanwhile, in the global South the carrier tricycle was to emerge as an efficient and flexible vehicle for local transportation. Yet many people in China and other developing countries are disinterested in this vehicle, viewing it as a superannuated mode of transport even though it meets many of the criteria important to civilisation.

References

Adams, J. (1999) "Hypermobility: the road to ruin", BBC News 11 December.

Adams, J. (2010) "Risk in a hypermobile world" http://john-adams.co.uk/10/2/2010.

Beck, U. (1992) *Risk Society: Towards a New Modernity* (London: Sage).

Beck, U. (2009 – translated by Ciaran Cronin) *World at Risk* (Cambridge: Polity Press).

Freud, S. (1929) *Civilisation and Its Discontents*. (re-published by Penguin: London in 2002).

Furness, Z. (2010) *One Less Car: Bicycling and the Politics of Automobility* (Philadelphia: Temple University Press).

Lemon, J. T. (1996) *Liberal Dreams and Nature's Limits: Great Cities of North America Since 1600* (Toronto: Oxford University Press).

Norcliffe, G. (2001) *The Ride to Modernity: The Bicycle in Canada 1869-1900* (Toronto: University of Toronto Press)

Norcliffe, G. (2006) "Associations, modernity and the insider-citizens of a Victorian highwheel bicycle club". *Journal of Historical Sociology*, Vol. 19, 121-150.

Norcliffe G. (2009) "G-COT: The geographical construction of technology". *Science, Technology and Human Values*, Vol. 34 (4), 449-475.

Stiglitz, J. E. (2002) *Globalization and its Discontents*. (New York: Norton).

DISCUSSION PAPER

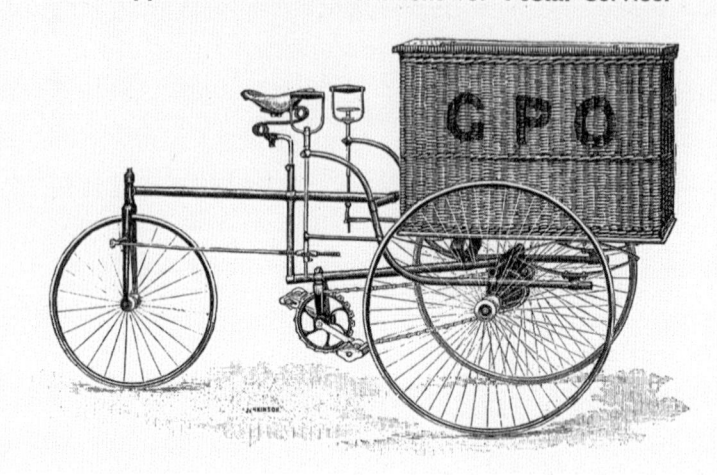

The Premier Carrier Tricycle equipped for the British General Post Office, 1886.
(Source: Hillman, Herbert and Cooper (1886) *Catalogue of Bicycles and Tricycles* (Coventry: Iliffe) (unpaginated))

Recycling in Zhou Zhuang, Jiangsu Province, China.
(photography by G. Norcliffe)

9. Finding a Place for Japanese and Chinese Cities within an East Asian Regional Urbanism

Paul Waley

1. Comparative Urbanism and Area Studies

My starting point for this inquiry lies in what I perceive to be a failure to integrate the study of urban change in Japan into a regional and an international comparative context. The questions I raise here connect Japanese to Chinese cities and anchor them in the East Asian region. They relate not only to Japanese and Chinese cities and their regional context but also to wider questions of convergence and difference -- the extent to which claims can be made for an urban convergence orchestrated by global capital. My principal argument is that a comparative study of urban change in Japan and China is mutually beneficial, and enhances the study of urbanism in the East Asian region and beyond[1]. More broadly, I argue that elements of urban change in China and Japan can be seen to make up a regional variant and a regional response to the commodification and globalization of the urban environment. Clearly, China is central within the East Asian region, and, as I hope to show, there is much to be gained from a specific comparative focus on Japanese and Chinese urbanism.

My interest was originally stimulated by the work of Terry McGee (1991) and his delineation of areas of mixed urban and rural activities around and between large East and Southeast Asian cities which he called *desakota*, using the Malay/Indonesian words for a village and a town. McGee was responding to a sense of the need to find an appropriate theoretical setting for the distinctive quality of urban change in East and Southeast Asia. McGee's theory was subsequently criticized for perpetuating a myth both of the continued validity of the Southeast Asian city per se and of the Southeast Asian city as Third World City. In their critique of *desakota* Dick and Rimmer (1998) argued that in an age of global convergence urban form and lifestyles in Southeast Asia were shaped by the same forces as those in North America. There have been various subsequent contributions to the debate, with Ma and Wu (2005) critical of what they see as Dick and Rimmer's implicit alignment of globalization with homogenization.

The argument that something called Southeast Asian cities should not be conflated with something else called Third World Cities is surely compelling and is part of an intellectual attack on the validity of the notion of TWCs. It is equally compelling to insist that Southeast Asian cities should be studied within the context of urbanism worldwide. However, the concept of *desakota* included densely populated parts of Japan, South Korea, Taiwan, and China and so was clearly built around distinctive features of regional urbanism rather than a model that could be applied indiscriminately throughout the Third World. Two interesting and closely related issues arise from this discussion: the validity of area studies and the interplay between global convergence and local difference.

These are issues with a strong resonance in recent literature that links debates in urban studies (Amin and Graham, 1997) and develops the idea of ordinary cities (Robinson, 2002) to encompass postcolonial concepts of cosmopolitan urbanism (Legg and McFarlane, 2008). The thrust behind much of this writing is a move away from the fixed positions and false dichotomies of modernity—modern against primitive and theory-rich urban studies versus theory-poor development studies. As McFarlane (2008, 355) writes, "This requires that we think carefully about the play of the general and particular in the production of theory, so that case studies are not 'added-on' to a given theoretical position and understood narrowly through the trope of copy/unique." The literature is animated by a sense that urban studies is innately comparative and that this needs to be recognized, but that comparative urbanism needs to be informed by a cosmopolitan sensitivity, sensitive to context and built on an understanding of relevant historical threads. A strong case has been made for this approach to comparative urbanism in a European context (Bodnár, 2001; Le Galès, 2002). But any such comparative work needs to be both highly sensitive to difference yet bold enough to contemplate generalization (Ma, 2002).

One of the aims of this paper is to suggest ways in which comparative study of Chinese and Japanese cities within an East Asian regional context can help resolve the tension between sensitivity to difference and the need to generalize in order to transcend specificities and tell stories that have wider meaning. This is predicated on a rich understanding of the regional context, and indeed it is the regional focus that opens up possibilities for a more sensitive understanding of convergence and difference. In other words, I am advocating here a reassessment of the conceptual mileage that can be gained from area studies, in line with arguments recently advanced by Pollard *et al.* (2009). An area focus recognizes the historical weight that proximity has brought to bear in terms of human ties over a long period of time (Legg and McFarlane, 2008). It also facilitates a reading of links to global flows and trends that is more sensitive to local difference, and provides theoretical sustenance for a contextually sensitive understanding of region.

In this paper, I argue that three different types of comparative urbanism can be identified, each of which can be effective, but that it is work growing out of an understanding of regional context which has most to offer. Comparative urbanism can be systemic and convergent, making a case for global convergence. Or it can be strategic, comparing cities in different settings in order to make specific points, about governance, perhaps, or social segregation. Or it can be more contextually sensitive, designed to draw out difference in a more restricted regional context. It is precisely this sort of comparative urbanism that is being advocated here, not least because it affords the most robust basis for global-scale comparison. The paper continues with some reflections on different theoretical perspectives into which the comparative study of cities can be set. It sees developmental state theory as a route into a regional perspective from which a contextually sensitive comparative urbanism can be derived. Alongside this, the paper provides some examples of what I am calling here strategic comparative urbanism. In the short compass of this paper it is not possible to do anything more than allude to a few central themes. The possibilities for work comparing contemporary cities in Japan and China are examined in terms of urban governance, the urban landscape and the social geography of urban life. Finally, the argument is brought back into a broader regional context.

1 The East Asian region for present purposes consists of China (including Hong Kong), Taiwan, South Korea, and Japan. This is the region sometimes referred to as Northeast Asia. These territories are bound together not only by a shared culture (political culture, culture of writing, religious culture), but more importantly in this context by patterns of influence, empire, and investment. Not included in this reading of the East Asian region are the countries of Southeast Asia and their cities—Bangkok, Manila, Jakarta, etc. While there are many common strands—for example as a result of Japanese (and latterly Chinese) investment—historical influences in Southeast Asia have been somewhat different, and European (and American) colonial occupation has brought about divergent paths of urban change. Of course, this type of boundary drawing is intended only to be indicative. Singapore, for example, is normally seen as a developmental state, and as a city it probably has more in common with the cities of Northeast Asia, despite its colonial history. While these distinctions are important, it is equally important to avoid the sort of cultural determinism that informed much of the "Asian values" debate, according to which economic success in East Asia could be related to a set of values with a more or less Confucian heritage -- all of which was then peremptorily stood on its head at the time of the Asian Financial Crisis in 1997 and 1998 (Kelly and Olds, 1999).

2. The Academic Division of Labour

The call here is for a more sensitive contextual comparative urbanism, but the academic division of labour mitigates strongly against it. This was a point made some time ago by Anthony King: "The real divisions of scholarship, as well as the ideological underpinnings that help to keep them alive, ensure that histories of 'First'-, 'Second'-, and 'Third'-World cities are still kept tidily apart" (1990, 78). We are faced with what Pollard *et al.* (2009, 138) refer to as "a divisive geopolitics of knowledge."

The tendency has been for work on cities to remain immured within academic walls that have reflected different theoretical positions and detracted from a sensitive and contextual area studies approach to comparative urbanism. Urban studies and global cities specialists have concentrated on the cities of the First World while development specialists dealt with Third World cities. Chinese cities have tended to be the preserve of China specialists, and Japanese cities, all the more so of Japan specialists—their very specialisms acting as barriers to a regional focus. In itself, this is not surprising; development studies, although they have moved off the discursive ground of Third World Cities and onto the terrain of mega cities, still tend to concentrate on a range of urban features such as spontaneous settlements and, informal labor that are of some, if limited, relevance to the Chinese urban context (Ma, 2002) but of no relevance to Japan.

In recent years, however, a number of writers have set Chinese cities in particular and to a lesser extent Japanese cities within a wider comparative framework. One of the more systematic of these attempts was undertaken by John Logan and colleagues (Logan, 2008). In their introduction to this work, Logan and Fainstein asked contributors to find a theoretical fit for their own thematic studies. Contributors were asked to choose between modernization, dependency/world systems theory, developmental state theory, and post-socialist transition theory. Intriguingly, most authors found that the changing urban conditions they described failed to match neatly with any of these theoretical approaches. A few found aspects of all relevant and useful; others found little of use in any of them. Only developmental state theory appeared to offer some mileage, a point we shall return to shortly.

In fact the academic division of labour with its accompanying theoretical baggage, as outlined by Logan and Fainstein, calls for closer scrutiny. For a start, the four theoretical categories might usefully be reshuffled. Modernization theory in whichever of its two contemporary derivatives, globalization theory and development theory, follows a line of global convergence. Theories of post-socialist transition and the developmental state are built, as I shall argue below, on difference rather than convergence. World systems theory could be understood as a bridge between the two to the extent that it attempts to build an understanding of the contextualized development of global capital, ideas founded on the richly contextualized work of Braudel and Wallerstein.

As Laurence Ma (2002) has argued, convergence arguments have their place, so long as they are informed by and deployed alongside an understanding built through careful contextual study. This is most likely to issue from specialist area studies departments, but here a rich level of detail needs to be set against a broader theoretical grasp. The convergence-difference debate is all too easily reflected in a stand-off between the theory-driven generalist and the detail-obsessed specialist.

If King's "division of scholarship" embodied and reflected the fault line between the rich, first, global world and the poor, third, undeveloped world, Robinson more recently (2002, 533) has detected a "partial redressing of this divide…, especially within historical writing and a more culturally-inflected urban studies." To follow up Robinson's point, let us return briefly to Logan and Fainstein's list of theoretical approaches that might help to anchor a study of Chinese urbanism. The last two were theories of transition from socialism and developmental state theory. Both these theoretical positions allow for the building up of a rich contextual understanding anchored in a broader theoretical analysis.

For post-socialist (and transitional) urbanism to be of epistemological value, one must recognize the different trajectory being pursued by Central and Eastern European countries on the one hand and China and Vietnam on the other; only then does it becomes clear that the theoretical content of post-socialism is heavily inflected by regional context. Path dependence has emerged as a key concept in discussions of urban change in CEE countries (Szelenyi, 1996). This is related to a recognition that conditions in different cities in the region bore a number of differences before and during the period of socialism and these have affected directions since. Comparing trends in Chinese cities with developments in CEE becomes therefore an exercise in strategic comparison, primarily evoking contrast to prompt understanding. A review of recent literature on land, property and housing in China supports this point (see for example Logan *et al.*, 2009). But it is perhaps significant that one of the most controversial recent interventions evokes a broader European experience to bring greater clarity to theorization of land markets in China (Haila, 2007).

Developmental state theory is comparative by its very nature, and regional in its compass, and the region it encompasses is generally seen to consist of the territories that concern us here, Japan, Taiwan, and Korea, with the addition of Singapore. China today meets many of the relevant criteria of a developmental state (Stubbs, 2009). The assumptions behind developmental state theory are well-known and do not need a full recapitulation here (Wade, 1990; Woo-Cummings, 1999). They are built around a set of institutions and policy approaches that create a close and productive relationship between the state and capital. What has been little studied and discussed in the literature is the way in which the role of the state and capital and their close relationship has conditioned the nature, speed and shape of urban change. It is to this theme that the current paper is particularly addressed, and in this it is responding to a call made in a study which itself consists of a comparison of governance and local communities in China and Taiwan for "a more holistic understanding" of the developmental state that would "go beyond its economic dimensions [and] include urban governance" (Read and Chen, 2008, 331).

3. Japanese Cities and Comparative Urbanism

Central to my concerns here is a desire to establish a better contextual understanding of urban change in Japan, driven by a sense that only the East Asian region and China in particular provide a suitably rich body of material on which to base this understanding. It is worth noting, however, on the one hand that little attempt has been made to set Japanese cities within a regional context (and not much more so for Chinese cities). On the other hand, Tokyo has been inserted prominently into discussion about global convergence, most notably by John Friedmann (1986), Saskia Sassen (1991) and Peter Taylor (2000) in their work on world and global cities. And yet the Japanese capital sits uneasily in the set of hypotheses elaborated by these writers.

It is particularly relevant to the argument being advanced here that, in their critique of Friedmann's and Sassen's theoretical position, Hill and Kim emphasized the nature of the developmental state as a key determinant of urban change in Tokyo, and with it Seoul. Tokyo, they argued, is not like New York "market-centred and bourgeois [but] state-centred and political-bureaucratic" (2000, 2168). The bureaucracy occupies centre stage; risk-takers on the markets are secondary players. Manufacturing is a key motor driving the economy of these cities, as much as finance and other high order service industries. In social terms, both Tokyo and Seoul, as well as Shanghai, have a much less heterogeneously composed population than either New York or London. The regional arena, they are saying, is much more fruitful for comparative urbanism than is the global, systemic one.

To say this is neither to deny that convergent comparative work is of value nor to suggest that only regional and contextual comparison should be undertaken. Indeed, the most rewarding comparative work involving Japanese cities has been strategic in its scope, contrasting developments in Japan and in the West to advance a specific argument (and the same is true of some recent work on Chinese cities; see for example various chapters in Logan, 2008, and Chen, 2009). Thus Forrest and Hirayama (2009) contrast housing policy in Britain and Japan to create a clearer picture of the impact of neoliberal housing policies in the two countries. Jacobs (2003) has contrasted governmental policies at different scales in the Detroit and Nagoya regions to argue for the greater effectiveness of Japanese-style integrated policies. Fielding (2004) has produced evidence to argue that social segregation, while apparent in a Japanese city like Kyoto, is nonetheless not as significant as it is in a British city like Edinburgh. There is surely much to be gained from this sort of strategic comparison. Issues of expertise, which all too easily become a real barrier to contextually rich urban comparison (Ma, 2002; Pollard *et al.*, 2009), can be overcome through the combined use of expert knowledge in the two different geographical areas or through recourse to local "home-based" accretions of understanding. Indeed, if we accept my categorization of comparative urban work into convergent, strategic and contextual, then in the case of Japanese cities it is probably the case that it is in the strategic mode that the most fruitful studies have been carried out.

4. Comparing Japanese and Chinese Cities

Any engagement with the comparative study of Japanese and Chinese cities needs to be grounded in history, and to reflect the influence of Japan on Chinese urban modernization both as 'benign' educator of intellectuals and incubator of concepts and as 'malign' imperial force. The constraints of space however limit the present text to a discussion of developments over the last few decades. In both Japan and China, the state has engineered changes—in property ownership rights in the case of China and zoning regulations in the case of Japan—to create propitious conditions for the exploitation of the urban terrain. In both countries, urban development capital has created highly dynamic, plastic urban environments. And in both countries, loose planning regulations have greatly facilitated the globalization of urban space, with master planning being little more than indicative (Yeh, 2005). Japan has experienced three turbulent decades during which property prices have quadrupled, fallen to their original level, and then risen again (Waley, 2007). During this period the urban landscape of major cities has been altered beyond recognition through an explosion of high-rise buildings. If Japan has experienced tumultuous urban change in the last few decades, this is all the more the case in China. The state, both national and local, has guided the marketization of land and commodification of property, using a dual system to marketize land, through leasing and allocation. The leasing of urban land has been of prime importance in generating the necessary capital to improve infrastructure and thus help generate more capital accumulation from land (Wu, 2009). In recent years, the central state, having released energies at the local municipal level, has been attempting to re-assert control through measures designed to re-establish a greater degree control over the urban restructuring process (Xu et al., 2009).

I will suggest two areas that could benefit from comparative investigation. One is the nature and role of neighborhood organizations in Chinese and Japanese cities; the other is the series of policies adopted by local governments in cities like Tokyo and Shanghai to support small-scale manufacturers. The urban landscapes of Chinese and Japanese cities have both been shaped as a result of their penetration by extractive capital—that is to say, by large corporations, investment companies, private developers, specialist property companies, all involved in extracting profit from the urban terrain. Here, I will refer briefly to the way in which the existence of urban compounds, often holdovers from the previous 'high-modernist' historical period, has facilitated the conversion of previously horizontal cities into cities with large clusters of skyscrapers.

Neighborhood organizations retain a relatively significant role within many parts of Chinese and Japanese cities. Both the residents committees (*jumin weiyuanhui*) of Chinese cities and the neighborhood associations (*chōnaikai* and *jichikai*) in urban areas in Japan remain durable institutions with a role that bridges the gap between the household and the lowest tier of local government (Pekkanen, 2006; Read and Chen, 2008). The interplay of influences not only between Japan and China but also involving Korea and Taiwan has been complex. Premodern systems of community organization and surveillance existed in Japan, Korea, and

China. Later the Japanese used a version of neighborhood associations in much of their empire both to promote urban hygiene and to enforce social control. But, as Read and Chen argue, the continued strength of locality-based community organizations is a regional phenomenon, and one that needs to be examined and discussed in the context of the developmental state.

Both Tokyo and Shanghai include extensive industrial areas where manufacturing remains an important function. Yangpu District in the north of Shanghai and Sumida Ward in east Tokyo have a history as centers of urban industrial production. In both district and ward (and this applies to other adjacent wards in Tokyo) residential land use has increased significantly (Zhang, 2005). In the industrial east of Tokyo, many larger factories were relocated as early as the 1960s and 1970s, but ward offices have since fought a rearguard action over a long period to help retain a favorable working environment for small-scale manufacturers, of whom a significant number remain, even as they have sought to create an environment more amenable to residents. On the other hand, Yangpu District "has made efforts to diversify its economic base" (Zhang, 2005, p. 182), but with mixed results.

Urban landscapes have changed vertiginously in China and in Japan in the last three decades. One conspicuous feature of the urban landscape that has facilitated this transformation is the compound, understood here as a large, fenced-off plot of land with a common history of use. Compounds have been a distinctive feature of the Chinese urban landscape for a long time (Bray, 2005; Lu, 2006). The form of contemporary urban development in China still tends to reflect this, as the sites of work unit compounds (many of them factories and associated social facilities) are converted into apartment blocks or commercial buildings. Some of the larger compounds of pre-modern Japanese cities later became factories and railway yards; many of these have since been transformed into high-rise urban development projects.

Both Chinese and Japanese cities had until very recently been almost completely horizontal. They now contain large and growing numbers of skyscrapers, a few of them landmark buildings designed by international architects (Olds, 2001; Gaubatz, 2005). In both countries the surge in extractive urban development that occurred—starting in the early 1980s in Japan, about a decade later in China—reflected decisions taken by central governments and enthusiastically endorsed by city governments to make land a basis for capital accumulation, and the easiest way to do this was to release large plots, or compounds, onto the market. There are to be sure many differences, in mechanisms of land disposal and in streams of capital accumulation. But in each case, as I have already suggested, strategic decisions were taken to use land to generate income, for the state in China and for business interests in Japan.

What has been the impact of this dramatic transformation of the urban landscape on urban life-spaces in China and Japan? As the skyscrapers have shot upwards, the global office functions and elite production and consumption services that fill them have spread outwards. This expansion of global business and related functions into inner city areas has created social tensions in both Chinese and Japanese cities. In the latter case these have been muted and under-studied (but see Sorensen *et al*, 2010). In the former case, very considerable numbers of people have been removed from old inner city housing to new housing estates, some in situ, most in suburban areas (Broudehoux, 2004; 2007). The resulting dislocation has been in part mitigated by improved housing conditions and rising living standards.

It is likely too that low levels of spatial segregation in the largest cities of both countries have played their part. The absence of large geographical concentrations of poverty has arguably eased pressures and restricted the possibilities for a coordination of expressions of resentment. During the industrial, high-modernist period in Japanese cities, in the first half of the twentieth century in particular, pockets of poverty existed here and there, in the south of Osaka and the east of Tokyo, for example. These pockets of poverty were generally to be found in industrial districts near waterways. They took the form of sub-standard wooden terraced housing, often located on plots owned by a single landlord. Nowadays, a few pockets of poverty still exist in the form of districts where day laborers and the elderly homeless congregate. At a more general level, disparities in wealth are demarcated on the urban terrain, but there is some disagreement about their extent and nature (Fujita and Hills, 1997; Fielding, 2004; Jacobs, 2005). Where poverty exists in Japanese cities (and recent OECD figures suggest that the prevalence of relative poverty is higher than is often thought [Nagata and Kiyokawa, 2009]), it tends to be spatially dispersed, hidden away at the household or individual level.

In China's case, spatial segregation, it has been argued, is found at a micro or neighborhood scale or even at the scale of the block. The "residential pattern is characterized by segregation at the micro-level (neighborhood) but mixing at the macro-level (city)" (Huang, 2005, p. 217). Neighborhood segregation in Chinese cities is primarily a function of unequal access to welfare, services, and housing. This stems from the attempt to control immigration into cities through a system of residence permits (*hukou*). No such system has existed in Japanese cities (at least not since the pre-modern period). There are, then, some notable differences. Yet urban life-spaces in China and Japan contain some similarities. In both Chinese and Japanese cities, there are relatively low levels of social tension, and therefore, we may assume, higher levels of social integration (Stanilov, 2007). This is despite the extremely dynamic and plastic nature of the urban landscape, which is being transformed rapidly from a horizontal to a vertical environment as a result of the vigorous flow of capital operating on the urban terrain, incentivized by supportive state policies.

5. Re-discovering East Asian Urban Affinities

In both China and Japan, the state has initiated and directed policy changes that have promoted the commodification of urban space and has in various ways choreographed its globalization. Japanese capital has been well placed to take advantage of the new regulatory climate created by the state, while in China, overseas Chinese and other global interests have been drawn in. This rapport between state and capital reverberates beyond Japan and China. Japanese, Chinese, Taiwanese, and Korean capital has been a strong driver of urban change in Southeast Asia. And yet, urban development capital and the social changes it engenders both in the "classic" East Asian region and beyond it in Southeast Asia are factors largely absent from developmental state theorizing.

Southeast Asia has of course above all been the recipient of large investments in manufacturing from Japan, South Korea, Taiwan, and now Chinese interests. But there are further types of investment, which have remained largely unreported, that help to illustrate how East Asian urbanism more generally has spread into and influenced the development trajectories of Southeast Asian countries. Important influences and investments have been projected through the practices of planning and construction (Rimmer, 1990). Aid policy and the activity of planning consultancies have played an important role in diffusing Japanese approaches to urbanization throughout Southeast Asia. South Korean companies have designed and built satellite cities in Indonesia (Dick and Rimmer, 1998) and now in Cambodia too. The export of Japanese goods and consumer tastes has been facilitated by the early establishment of Japanese department stores in cities such as Hong Kong and Singapore. While the export of "soft" Japanese (and more recently Korean) culture—electronic, animated, culinary, mediatic, etc.—has encouraged what Iwabuchi (2002) has described as a sort of Asian globalization.

It would of course be misguided to see the process as one way, southwards from the more prosperous northeast of Asia. Singaporean capital and capital emanating from overseas Chinese interests have powerfully pollinated urban growth throughout Southeast Asia. Indeed, property speculation was one of the ingredients in the crisis of 1997 and 1998, especially in Thailand. At a more general level, China's greater openness, especially to diaspora Chinese has encouraged a considerable degree of regional integration at a personal, cultural and economic level. Nor should one forget the institutional structures that operate throughout the wider region (Higgott, 1999).

The comparative study of changing urban conditions in China and Japan can surely contribute not only to an understanding of urban change in the East Asian region but to a wider appreciation of the social impact of urban restructuring and to a more complete theorization of the nature and role of the developmental state.

6. What Does Sino-Japanese Comparative Urbanism Tell Us about Globalization?

The nature of urban development capital differs in China and Japan, and the link to global capital differs too. In this sense, Ma and Wu have a point in dismissing "the much discredited notion of globalization-as-homogenization" (2005, 12) and rebutting arguments of global convergence. And yet at a different level, convergence there surely is. This can be seen in the internationalization of urban space in central and inner city areas causing a loss of distinctiveness in the urban landscape (Gaubatz 2005, 116). This inevitably impinges on the *sense* of the day-to-day urban experience in Japanese and Chinese cities. The landscapes of consumption that dominate Japanese and Chinese cities today are penetrated by both global and regional capital (more so, as we have seen, in the Chinese case). And created thus is a regional variant (but only a variant) to rampant commodification and globalization of the urban environment—and a distinctively regional response to global capital penetration.

Where should we look for this regional variant? We should look in the dynamic nature of Sino-Japanese urban change, driven by the close relationship between the state and capital and manifested in particular through the rapid conversion of central and inner districts from a horizontal to a vertical landscape. We should look in the tendency for social tensions resulting from this rapidly changing urban landscape to be underplayed, concealed from wider society. And we should look in the continued pattern of social segregation that shows itself at a micro rather than a macro level, and in the potentially related issue of the persistent existence and effectiveness of a number of locality-based institutions of community governance. In East Asia, the globalization of the urban environment is inflected by regional variants and coloured by regional responses.

References

Amin, A., and Graham, S., 1997, The ordinary city. *Transactions of the Institute British Geographers* Vol. 22, No. 4, 411–429.

Bodnár, J., 2001, *Fin de Millénaire Budapest: Metamorphoses of Urban Life*. Minneapolis, MN: University of Minnesota Press.

Bray, D. 2005. *Social Space and Governance in Urban China: The Danwei System from Origins to Reform*. Stanford, CA: Stanford University Press.

Broudehoux, A-M., 2004, *The Making and Selling of Post-Mao Beijing*. London: Routledge.

Broudehoux, A-M., 2007, Spectacular Beijing: The conspicuous construction of an Olympic Metropolis. *Journal of Urban Affairs*, Vol. 29, No. 4, 383–399.

Chen, X., editor, 2009. *Shanghai Rising: State Power and Local Transformations in a Global Megacity*. Minneapolis: U of Minnesota Press.

Dick, H., and Rimmer, P. J., 1998, Beyond the Third World City: The new urban geography of South-east Asia. *Urban Studies*, Vol. 35, No.12, 2303–2321.

Fielding, A., 2004, Class and space: Social segregation in Japanese cities. *Transactions of the Institute of British Geographers* Vol. 29, No. 1, 64–84.

Forrest, R., and Hirayama, Y., 2009, The uneven impact of neoliberalism on housing opportunities. *International Journal of Urban and Regional Research* Vol. 33, No. 4, 998–1013.

Friedmann, J., 1986, The World City hypothesis. *Development and Change* Vol. 17, No. 1, 60–83.

Fu, Z., 2002, The state, capital, and urban restructuring in post-reform Shanghai. In J. Logan, editor, *The New Chinese City: Globalization and Market Reform*. Oxford: Blackwell, 106–120.

Fujita, K., and Hill, R. C., 1997. Together and Equal: Place Stratification in Osaka. In P. P. Karan and K. Stapleton, editors, *The Japanese City*. Lexington: University Press of Kentucky, 105–128.

Gaubatz, P., 2005, Globalization and the development of new central business districts in Beijing, Shanghai and Guangzhou. In L. Ma and F. Wu, editors, *Restructuring the Chinese City: Changing Economy Society and Space*. London: Routledge, 98–121.

Haila, A., 2007, The market as the new emperor. *International Journal of Urban and Regional Research*, Vol. 31, No.1, 2241–2256.

Higgott, R., 1999, The political economy of globalisation in East Asia: The salience of 'region building.' In K. Olds, P. Dicken, P. E. Kelly, L. Kong, and H. Yeung, editors, *Globalisation and the Asia-Pacific: Contested Territories*. London: Routledge, 91–106.

Hill, R. C., and Kim, J. W., 2000, Global cities and developmental states: New York, Tokyo and Seoul. *Urban Studies*, Vol. 12, No. 1, 2167–2195.

Huang, Y., 2005, From work-unit compounds to gated communities: Housing inequality and residential segregation in transitional Beijing. In L. Ma and F. Wu, editors, *Restructuring the Chinese City: Changing Economy Society and Space*. London: Routledge, 192–221.

Huang, Y., and Jiang, L., 2009, Housing Inequality in Transitional Beijing. *International Journal of Urban and Regional Research*, Vol. 33, No. 4, 936–956.

Iwabuchi, K., 2002, *Recentering Globalization: Popular Culture and Japanese Transnationalism*. Durham: Duke University Press.

Jacobs, A., 2003, Embedded autonomy and uneven metropolitan development: A comparison of the Detroit and Nagoya auto regions, 1969–2000. *Urban Studies*, Vol. 40, No. 2, 335–360.

Jacobs, A., 2005, Has central Tokyo experienced uneven development? An examination of Tokyo's 23 *ku* relative to America's largest urban centers. *Journal of Urban Affairs*, Vol. 27, No. 5, 521–555.

Kelly, P. E., and Olds, K., 1999, Questions in a crisis: The contested meanings of globalisation in the Asia-Pacific. In K. Olds, P. Dicken, P. E. Kelly, L. Kong, and H. Yeung, editors, *Globalisation and the Asia-Pacific: Contested Territories*. London:

Routledge, 1–16.

King, A., 1990, *Urbanism, Colonialism, and the World-Economy: Cultural and Spatial Foundations of the World Urban System*. London: Routledge.

Legg, S., and McFarlane, C., 2008, Ordinary urban spaces: Between postcolonialism and development. *Environment and Planning A*, Vol. 40, No.1, 6–14.

Logan, J., editor, 2008, *Urban China in Transition*. Oxford: Blackwell.

Logan, J., and Fainstein, S., 2008, Introduction: Urban China in comparative perspective. In J. Logan, editor. *Urban China in Transition*. Oxford: Blackwell. 1–22.

Logan, J., Fang, Y., and Zhang, Z., 2009, Access to housing in urban China. *International Journal of Urban and Regional Research* Vol. 33, No. 4, 914–935.

Lu, D., 2006, *Remaking Chinese Urban Form: Modernity, Scarcity and Space*, 1949-2005. London: Routledge.

Ma, L., and Wu F., 2005, Restructuring the Chinese city: Diverse processes and reconstituted spaces. In L. Ma and F. Wu, editors, *Restructuring the Chinese City: Changing Economy Society and Space*. London: Routledge, 1–20.

Ma, L., 2002, Urban transformation in China, 1949 - 2000: A review and research agenda. *Environment & Planning A*, Vol. 34, No. 9, 1545–1569.

McFarlane, C., 2008, Urban shadows: Materiality, the 'southern city' and urban theory. *Geography Compass*, Vol. 2, No. 2, 340–358.

McGee, T., 1991, The emergence of *desakota* regions in Asia: Expanding a hypothesis. In N. Ginsburg, B. Koppel, and T. McGee, editors, *The Extended Metropolis: Settlement Transition in Asia*. Honolulu: University of Hawaii Press, 3–25.

Nagata, T., and Kiyokawa, T., 2009, Ministry now grappling with startling poverty rate. *The Asahi Shimbun*, 2 December. Accessed from:
http://www.asahi.com/english/Herald-asahi/TKY200912020130.html

Olds, K., 2001, *Globalization and Urban Change: Capital, Culture, and Pacific Rim Mega-Projects*. Oxford: Oxford University Press.

Pekkanen, R., 2006, *Japan's Dual Civil Society: Members without Advocates*. Stanford, CA: Stanford University Press.

Pollard, J., McEwan, C., Laurie, N., and Stenning, A., 2009, Economic geography under postcolonial scrutiny. *Transactions of the Institute of British Geographers*, Vol. 34, No. 2, 137–142.

Read, B. I., and Chen, C. M., 2008, The state's evolving relationship with urban society: China's neighborhood organizations in comparative perspective. In J. Logan, editor, *Urban China in Transition*. Oxford: Blackwell, 315–335.

Rimmer, P. J., 1990, The internationalisation of Japanese construction firms: The rise and rise of Kumagai Gumi *Environment and Planning A*, Vol. 22, No. 3, 346–368.

Robinson, J., 2002, Global and world cities: A view from off the map. *International Journal of Urban and Regional Research*, Vol. 26, No. 2, 531–554.

Robinson, J., 2004, In the tracks of comparative urbanism: Difference, urban modernity and the primitive. *Urban Geography*, Vol. 25, No. 8, 709–723.

Saitō, A., and Thornley, A., 2003, Shifts in Tokyo's world city status and the urban planning response. *Urban Studies*, Vol. 40, No. 4, 665–685.

Sassen, S., 1991, *The Global City: New York, London, Tokyo*. Princeton, N.J.: Princeton University Press.

Stanilov, K., editor, 2007, *The Post-Socialist City: Urban Form and Space Transformation in Central and Eastern Europe after Socialism*. Dordrecht: Springer.

Stubbs, R., 2009, Whatever happened to the East Asian Developmental State? The unfolding debate. *Pacific Review*, Vol. 22, No. 1, 1–22.

Szelenyi, I., 1996, Cities under socialism—and after. In G. Andrusz, M. Harloe, and I. Szelenyi, editors. *Cities After Socialism:*

Urban and Regional Change and Conflict in Post-Socialist Societies. Oxford: Blackwell.

Taylor, P., 2000, World cities and territorial states under conditions of contemporary globalization. *Political Geography*, Vol. 19, No. 1, 5–32.

Wade, R. 1990. *Governing the Market: Economic Theory and the Role of Government in East Asian Industrialization*. Princeton, N.J.: Princeton University Press.

Waley, P., 2007, Tokyo-as-world-city: Reassessing the role of capital and the state in urban restructuring. *Urban Studies*, Vol. 44, No. 8, 1465–1490.

White, J., 1998, Old wine, cracked bottle? Tokyo, Paris and the global city hypothesis. Urban *Affairs Review*, Vol. 33, No. 4, 451–477.

Woo-Cumings, M., editor. 1999. *The Developmental State*. Ithaca, N.Y.: Cornell University Press.

Wu, F., 2009, Globalization, the changing state, and local governance in Shanghai. In X. Chen, editor, *Shanghai Rising: State Power and Local Transformations in a Global Megacity*. Minneapolis, MN: University of Minnesota Press, 125–144.

Yeh, A. G. O., 2005, Dual land market and internal spatial structure of Chinese cities. In L. Ma and F. Wu, editors, *Restructuring the Chinese City: Changing Economy Society and Space*. London: Routledge, 59–79.

Yin, H., Shen, X., and Zhao, Z., 2005, Industrial restructuring and urban spatial transformation in Xi'an. In L. Ma and F. Wu, editors, *Restructuring the Chinese City: Changing Economy Society and Space*. London: Routledge, 155–174.

Xu, J., Yeh, A., and Wu, F., 2009. Land commodification: New land development and politics in China since the late 1990s. *International Journal of Urban and Regional Research* Vol. 33, No. 4, 890–913.

10. Mediating a Global Network in Crisis: *The New York Times* Maps the Moral Geography of Global Finance

Gordon M. Winder

The global financial crisis may have significant effects on the position of New York City in financial networks and we should expect that this would be a matter of discussion in the city's leading daily newspaper. New York City is an alpha++ global city (GaWC 2009) and enjoys centrality in the network of global cities. However, the global cities networks, the flows between cities, and New York's centrality in financial networks are all being transformed by the global financial crisis. So, in this paper I ask how *The New York Times* makes sense of New York City's changing position in global markets, the strategies and policies needed to keep New York City at the top of the hierarchy and the threats to its position.

Among its many other functions and in competition with *The Wall Street Journal*, *The New York Times* maps the economic world for New Yorkers. It enjoys a readership including ordinary New Yorkers, cosmopolitan residents, workers on Wall Street, in the United Nations, and Fortune 500 company head offices, and a readership spread out through New York and other Northeast states. Its subventions, *The International Herald Tribune* and on-line versions are available for travellers and a European readership. Times Square is its iconic landmark, and *The New York Times* is well known as the reliable newspaper of record in the USA. Its economic reporting includes news of trading on New York stock exchanges, reports on company performance and business news, as well as reports and commentary on the US economy, trade and world business. It sources reports from many experts and includes opinion pieces by established economists. In these circumstances, it is not clear how global city networks figure in the newspaper's pages and it may be that other economic entities -- especially national and city economies -- are given more attention.

This paper assumes that *The New York Times* can be understood in part as a map: the daily newspaper uses geographical imaginaries, place references and a special sense of place to communicate the news. Building on the work of Benedict Anderson (1983), David Harvey (2000) and Derek Gregory (2004), it assumes that modern newspapers like *The New York Times* build imagined communities of readers, partly by printing geographical imaginaries that bind together the readership and distant places. Indeed, in the nineteenth century the modern newspaper invented a new sense of place and mediated specific civic rituals -- for example sales at department stores, commemorative services, arrivals and departures of ships, or fund-raising campaigns for the victims of disasters -- through which readers could virtually inhabit the distant places where great affairs take place, and engage with distant others (Rantanen 2003, Cottle 2006, Winder 2010). As Barnhurst and Nerone (2001) find, the modern newspaper claimed to map the social world for readers. It reported to them the happenings in their city and around the world, the new fashions and technologies, the new galleries, and tourism destinations. It operated as an agent for ever changing modernities. Not only can we identify the global mediascapes (Appadurai 1996) within which the newspaper is published, but also the geographical imaginaries and imagined communities constructed through its pages. What meanings does *The New York Times* ascribe to Wall Street, New York's financial industry, and New York City's imagined networks during the global financial crisis?

To answer this question, this paper uses *The New York Times* on-line database. Using the key words 'global financial crisis,' a search of the database for the two week period February 12-28, 2009 captured 21,289 words of text. These words were then analysed in terms of the place names, firms and actors referred to, the sources quoted, the economic theories and business terms used, and the narratives and interpretations discussed. I have not interviewed journalists or editors at *The New York Times*, nor do I endeavour to identify an editorial policy or interpretative thrust in my analysis. Indeed, I cannot, and do not, claim to have analysed the newspaper's coherent position on the global financial crisis, if such a thing were able to be identified. I accept that there are gatekeepers selecting the news that will appear, that editors of *The New York Times* exercise some influence on how the news is written, and that the finished online 'news' that I analyse is not only the outcome of many decisions and much work, but is also but one manifestation of the news on the global financial crisis from the media company that produces *The New York Times*. Rather, my aim is to identify the imagined position of New York in financial networks during the global financial crisis as told in various news stories printed in *The New York Times*. At best my aim is tentative: I hope to sketch in the geographical imaginaries and the narratives about the global financial crisis that were printed as the basis for some preliminary conclusions about imaginative geographies of New York City and Wall Street.

1. The Place Names and Actors of the Global Financial Crisis

An image of a trader standing in front of computer screens at a stock exchange in China (Hong Kong) tells the story that "markets in Europe and Asia (closed) lower on Monday" (Reuters, *NYT* February 16, 2009). But while other cities and countries figure in the news, this turns out to be a select set of such places, not coincident with the GaWC list of global cities (Table 1). In addition to the 19 references to Wall Street in those 21,289 words, only 20 cities are referred to in these two weeks. Six US cities (New York, Washington DC, Detroit, Chicago, Orlando and Las Vegas), account for 70 percent of all references and New York City alone for 60 percent. Bangkok, London, Baghdad, Singapore, Paris, Berlin, Tokyo and Hong Kong are each mentioned at least twice and together account for 37 of the 143 references. Beijing, Jakarta, Frankfurt, Kiev, Bucharest and Vienna are each mentioned once. However, some leading global cities, notably Shanghai and

Table 1 CITIES NAMED			
Named City	**References (no.)**	**GaWC Category**
New York	87	Alpha++
London	7	Alpha++
Singapore	5	Alpha+
Paris	4	Alpha+
Tokyo	2	Alpha+
Hong Kong	2	Alpha+
Beijing	1	Alpha+
Bangkok	8	Alpha-
Chicago	2	Alpha-
Jakarta	1	Alpha-
Frankfurt	1	Alpha-
Vienna	1	Alpha-
Washington DC	5	
Baghdad	5	
Detroit	4	
Berlin	4	
Orlando	1	
Las Vegas	1	
Kiev	1	
Bucharest	1	
Total	**143**	
Cities ranked by GaWC but not named by *NYT*: Shanghai, Sydney (Alpha+), Buenos Aires, Toronto, Brussels, Madrid, Milan, Moscow, Mumbai, Kuala Lumpur, Seoul (Alpha), Caracas, Mexico, Sao Paulo, Amsterdam, Athens, Budapest, Dublin, Istanbul, Lisbon, Prague, Rome, Stockholm, Warsaw, Zurich, Taipei, Auckland (Alpha-). **Source:** *New York Times* February 2009		

Sydney, and all of those located in the Americas outside the USA are not referred to at all. While the pattern of reporting using country reports to highlight issues and trends in broad regions gives pause for caution -- perhaps the equivalent stories from Africa, India, China or Latin America were published in the next weeks -- in fact the newspaper appears to relate stories of a network of US, European and Pacific Asian cities, that is a sub-set of the global cities list.

That tentative finding is confirmed by analysis of the authorities cited in the news. In reporting the global financial crisis *The New York Times* cites many authorities. Analysts, government officials, bankers, brokers, economists and CEOs are quoted, experts are reported and data and interpretation is referenced to specific agencies. By mapping these references we can sketch the extent of *The New York Times*' sources: who are the experts on the global economy and where are they based? In these two weeks government sources were particularly important and included President Obama, Ben Bernanke, Nicolas Sarkozy, Mayor Bloomberg and Iraqi ministers. Once again analysis reveals a specific geography, in this case, of expertise. One quarter of the references are to experts from New York City, another 12 percent from Washington DC, so that half of the locations cited are in the USA (Table 2). By sourcing expertise in Baghdad, Bangkok, Hong Kong, Tokyo and Thailand 20 times, the pattern of global city connections between New York and East and Southeast Asian and Iraqi cities is reinforced. The other experts are in Western European capitals. So, for example, although it reports on trade data from Brazil, Russia, India and China, *The New York Times* cites no authorities in these countries on that trade data. There appears to be a network of experts within the global cities network that *The New York Times* relates to its readers.

There are about the same number of references (135) to specific countries as there are to specific cities. Only 43 countries are mentioned (Table 3). Together, just four coun-

Table 2
AUTHORITIES CITED

Location	References (No.)
Boston	1
Chicago	1
Detroit	7
Las Vegas	1
New York	20
Washington DC	11
USA	**41**
Baghdad	4
Bangkok	4
Berlin	1
Brussels	1
Geneva	1
Hong Kong	2
London	3
Luxembourg	1
Paris	4
Thailand	3
Tokyo	7
Foreign	**31**
Unspecified	7
Total	**79**

Source: *New York Times* February 2009

Table 3
COUNTRIES NAMED

Country	References (No.)	(%)	Country	References (No.)	(%)
USA	26	9,6	Argentina	2	
Austria	1		Brazil	3	
Britain	3		Chile	2	
France	5		Mexico	1	3,0
Germany	8		Afghanistan	1	
Greece	1		Iraq	23	
Iceland	5		Saudi Arabia	1	9,3
Italy	1		India	3	1,1
Netherlands	1		China	7	2,6
Spain	3		Japan	32	
Sweden	1		South Korea	4	
Switzerland	1	11,1	Taiwan	2	14,1
Belarus	1		Cambodia	1	
Czech Rep.	3		Hong Kong	2	
Hungary	7		Indonesia	3	
Latvia	5		Laos	1	
Poland	6		Malaysia	22	
Romania	3		Philippines	52	
Serbia	1		Singapore	5	
Ukraine	3	10,7	Thailand	13	36,7
Russia	2	0,7	Australia	2	
			New Zealand	1	1,1
Source: *NYT* February 2009			**Total**	**270**	**100,0**

tries, Japan, the USA, Iraq and Thailand, account for two thirds of all country references. Iraq and the USA are said to be "intertwined," their futures and government budgets inseparable. Thailand's is the 'worst-hit' economy in South East Asia and Japan's is now the 'most damaged' economy. These cases highlight a pattern of in-depth reporting of specific national economies, each pegged as a worst case. Their performance is then used as a benchmark to compare the performance of other national economies.

In addition a number of formal regions are named (Table 4). Most of these names are for parts of Europe. Together, they account for over 70 percent of all the formal region names used. Perhaps unintentionally, this raises the issue of how many names are required to express the diverse European entities. By referring to the Euro-denominated economies, the 12, Western Europe, Eastern Europe and other names, the newspaper insinuates a fragmentation and lack of coherent leadership that is difficult for Americans to comprehend. How many names do we need for Europe? Thus the use of formal region names points to the lack of political cohesion in 'Europe.'

Table 4 FORMAL REGIONS NAMED	
Region Name	**References (No.)**
North America	3
Latin America	1
Asia	7
South East Asia	8
Europe	18
European Union	7
Euro zone	5
European bloc	1
European countries	2
Western Europe	1
Central and Eastern Europe	8
Eastern Europe	11
Baltic countries	2
G7	3
G20	1
Total	**78**
Source: *New York Times* February 2009	

Informal region names are also used. While references to Europe are more common than any one of these categories, three types of vaguely-specified regions are used as basic geographical imaginaries in the news of the global financial crisis. What I call 'global regions' refer to the integration of parts or all of the global economy. Such regions include 'tax havens,' the 'Trans-Atlantic money market,' the 'world trading system,' 'globalization' or the 'global economy.' There are 27 references to such regions, each of which implies a form of economic integration that is international and not easily captured by national or political names. This usage indicates the scope of the global economy imaginary, which in this case registers primarily as a constellation of North Atlantic economic activity. 'Divisional regions' refer to emerging, more or less developed or industrial economies. Crucial for comparative purposes, these regions are used to refer loosely to the separate categories of national economies. The 19 references to such divisions of the global economy indicate that such comparison and division remain an important element of *The New York Times*' geographical imagination. 'Emerging markets' are never clearly defined but their presence bolsters a particular developmentalist narrative of the world economy. 'Oppositional regions' refer to an opposing entity, the rest, those not defined by the characteristic referred to. There are 22 uses of such terms, including, for example, 'other former Soviet allies,' 'any other city than New York City,' and 'the local economy.' Sometimes this usage is used to signal uniqueness. At other times it registers that one example can stand for many others, since there is no substantive difference. These oppositional regions facilitate a form of abbreviation in that only a few specific cases are required to understand the patterns in the world economy.

In these two weeks *The New York Times* makes 190 references to 60 separate firms. Almost half of the firms referred to have their corporate head offices in New York City. Sixty-three percent of the enterprise references are to failed, failing or bailed out corporations. Together, references to Citigroup (26 percent), General Motors (4 percent), and Chrysler (7 percent) make up 37 percent of references. The bail-outs come from state-run banks (13 percent of references) including the World Bank, the International Monetary Fund and the European Investment Bank.

2. The Narratives of Global Financial Crisis even though 'America' is Seldom Used in This Context.

The loose key word proved useful, because, generally, *The New York Times* calls this problem a 'crisis' (40 references) rather than a 'bubble' (1), 'recession' (18) or other, less technical terms, (17) such as 'downturn.' Its usage of 'crisis' is often very specific: it is a credit, financial, banking or housing crisis. *The New York Times* refers to the globality of the crisis only 13 times. However, this count includes six references to 'world recession,' 'global downturn,' 'global economic slowdown,' 'global recession' and 'worldwide job cuts,' all signalling a shift in the crisis from the global financial sector to the world economy as a whole. In fact, *The New York Times* does not use the term 'global financial crisis' at all. Usually, the 'crisis' that it reports is an 'American' crisis even though 'American' is seldom used.

In these two weeks Mayor Bloomberg unveils the city's plans for Wall Street. One reference announces that Wall Street was about to "confound doomsayers" but the general impression left was that Wall Street was under threat, had suffered "a reversal of fortunes," and in the future would have "a smaller role in the city's economy." Indeed the city's financial sector was "haemorrhaging jobs," and "future jobs are not on Wall Street." In announcing the city's plans for the sector, Mayor Bloomberg pointedly declared that the "talented people coming out of Wall Street" needed to be "retrained," and that "a cultural and intellectual shift in thinking about Wall Street" was needed. Other references were less forgiving: 'Wall Streeters' are "guilty and being sentenced," they are "losers in the casinos of capitalism," or "defrocked wizards." In short, New York's financial sector was said to have lost credibility, in future it would have a smaller role in the city's economy, and Mayor Bloomberg looked to new ways to shore up city revenues. New York's global image needed to change: New York is a centre that welcomes entrepreneurs; New York's main asset is smart, ambitious, innovative people. Bloomberg drew these glib phrases from the report that he had received on New York City's future economy. In this re-imagining of New York City, Bloomberg reasserts that his city is the financial capital of the world set apart from its rivals, London, Beijing -- and MIT.

Two other political actors also give important speeches during these two weeks. President Obama delivers his State of the Union address. Federal Reserve Chairman, Ben Bernanke reports to the US Senate's banking committee. In his address to the nation, Obama necessarily declares the crisis to be a national one with national solutions. Obama's only references to other countries is his call for a full accounting of the costs of the USA's wars in Iraq and Afghanistan. Ben Bernanke focuses on the work of US Federal agencies dealing with the "financial crisis enveloping the country." He acknowledges the "global nature of the current economic slowdown," and refers to new risks emerging from offshore, but his main message is that there is no need to nationalize US banks.

There are "new risks for Wall Street as Eastern Europe falters." As currencies fall, demand contracts, and workers are laid off across the region, Ukrainians protest. Eastern European governments have big debts to Europe's banks and bailouts will be required. Readers are informed that Latvia is Europe's second collapsed government. The implications of these trends are registered with curious echoes of Cold War mentalities. These are "critical allies in the region embracing American-style capitalism and borrowing heavily from Western European banks." A photograph of Chinese workers camping near their country's embassy in Bucharest highlights the end to construction projects: some want help from the Chinese government to return to China.

Whether to nationalize Citigroup is apparently an important issue. The US Government raises its stake in Citigroup, which is "one of the nation's largest and most troubled financial institutions," and is "systematically critical." Citigroup reports a $27.7bn loss and its shares continue to fall. Washington is preparing to tighten its grip on Citigroup, but it is already calling many of the shots for the company. In reporting this bank's "third rescue," *The New York Times* notes that preferred stockholders, including "several foreign government investment funds" are invited to increase their stakes, but, this is a footnote to the issue of nationalization. Citigroup is portrayed as a US bank at risk of nationalization. The fact that Citigroup is partly owned by sovereign wealth funds is reported but remains incidental to the image of Citigroup as a US bank. The global interpenetration of investors' funds in the global banking group, Citigroup, may in fact be the key reason why the bank will not be nationalized; but this connection is not made explicit.

A series of reports use national trade data for January 2009 to show a dramatic fall in world trade. Data will not be available for the USA and many other national economies until March. In the absence of such data, the reports find that "highly globalized, small economies in East Asia" (Singapore, Hong Kong, Taiwan) are struggling as exports plunge. They are finding it hard to stimulate domestic demand. These are a special category of national economy and the implication is that these results are not the full picture and bear only partially on US trade data. Nevertheless, globalization is tied to vulnerability.

The New York Times reports on the effects of the crisis on interconnection with the rest of the world. Job losses, curbs on corporate spending and reduced trade show participation are noted. The reports relate to Las Vegas and are sourced from experts based in New York City. No national, international or New York City visitor numbers are given to support the news that job losses, curbs on corporate spending and reduced trade show participation are noted. Instead, the almost vacant registration area for a trade show in Las Vegas is photographed.

3. Conclusion

In the weeks February 12 to 28, 2009, *The New York Times* reports the state of national and city economies, not a global economy. The US and New York City economies will be restructured by their respective government administrations. New York City will pay the price of reduced employment: "Banks will be smaller and less profitable." Wall Street will be less important in the New York City economy, but there is no comment on the likely effects of the global financial crisis on New York City's global city ranking. The only attempt to express that impact is a statement about London, which is seen as a rival financial centre. In a curious twist on global interconnectedness and its implications, economist Simon Johnson declares that "It is one big Trans-Atlantic money market and these banks lend money to each other all the time." This statement seems to indicate that London and New York financial centres are interconnected, they will be equally impacted, and that therefore the rankings will be unaffected. In two other cases, similar logic is expressed. "Iraq and the USA are intertwined"; so, lower oil prices will impact on US-led reconstruction in Iraq. The "biggest US export is treasury bills" and the Obama administration needs to take into account that "foreigners are wary of long-term US securities." By drawing its comparisons with selected others, and by offering little or no commentary on Beijing, Shanghai, Delhi and so on, *The New York Times* at once makes this into a global crisis shared by all, and therefore unlikely to upset New York's status as the global financial capital, and a series of national crises requiring national solutions, rather than a global problem requiring international co-operation.

A moral geography is discernible in these pages of news. A global economic crisis is emerging. World trade, as reflected in national trade data, is down. Eastern Europe, Japan and South East Asia have trade and currency problems. Indeed, Eastern Europe has become "Europe's version of a subprime market." Other governments are active. So the global financial crisis is cast as a matter of national governments and their economies. In this situation, the federal administration in Washington DC is doing its job. Other governments are doing theirs. Thus, Obama's administration is insulated from responsibility for these foreign calamities. "Paying for other countries' mistakes is a European dilemma" and, implicitly, not a matter to trouble the US Government. Simon Johnson elaborates this moral geography of risk and responsibility: "We set off the dynamite, but a lot of people had tinderboxes under their houses." It is not really clear whether his 'we' refers to the USA, the Government in Washington DC, the Federal Reserve, or Wall Street brokers and bankers, though it is most likely the first of these. Just as an American problem requires an American solution, so other governments will need to be active and responsible. Nevertheless there is little news of inter-government co-operation, though Gordon Brown is due to arrive in Washington DC in March to make preparations for the next G20 meeting. Thus the global financial crisis is curiously less global, more keyed to national economies and national governments, and related less to global cities than might be expected. It seems that the circuits of capital that have been disrupted by the crisis are further disrupted by the geographical imaginaries that *The New York Times* and the experts that it quotes use to make sense of the crisis.

References

Anderson, B., 1983. *Imagined communities: Reflections on the origin and spread of nationalism.* London: Verso.

Appadurai, A., 1996. *Modernity at large: Cultural dimensions of globalization.* Minneapolis:University of Minnesota Press.

Barnhurst, K. G. and Nerone, J., 2001. *The form of the news: A history.* New York and London: Guilford Press.

Cottle, S., 2006. Mediatizing rituals: Beyond manufacturing consent. *Media, Culture and Society* 28(3): 411-432.

Gregory, D., 2004. *The colonial present.* Malden, Massachusetts: Blackwell.

Harvey, D., 2000. Cosmopolitanism and the banality of geographical evils. *Public Culture* 12(2): 529-564.

Rantanen, T., 2003. The new sense of place in nineteenth-century news. *Media, Culture and Society* 25: 435-449.

Winder, G. M., 2010. Imagining world citizenship in the networked newspaper: *La Nación* reports the assassination at Sarajevo, 1914. *Historical Social Research/Historische Sozialforschung* 35(1): 140-166.

URP GCOE DOCUMENT 11

Creating Cities;
Culture, Space and Sustainability:
The 1st City, Culture and Society (CCS) Conference

2012年2月
編集責任　Evelyn Schulz and Hiroshi Okano
発　　行　大阪市立大学 都市研究プラザ

大阪市立大学 都市研究プラザ
〒558-8585
大阪市住吉区杉本 3-3-138
電話 06-6605-2071　FAX06-6605-2069
URL www.ur-plaza.osaka-cu.ac.jp

本ドキュメントは文部科学省グローバル COE プログラム「文化創造と社会的包摂に向けた都市の再構築」の支援を受けたものである。

© 2012 Urban Research Plaza, Osaka City University

ISBN 978-4-88065-287-0　C3036

Printed in Japan

発売所 株式会社 水曜社
〒160-0022
東京都新宿区新宿 1-14-12
電話 03-3351-8768　FAX03-5362-7279
URL www.bookdom.net/suiyosha/